C000259289

100 Tips For Keyboards

You Should Have Been Told PART 1

Printed in the United Kingdom by MPG Books Ltd, Bodmin

Published by SMT, an imprint of Sanctuary Publishing Limited, Sanctuary House, 45–53 Sinclair Road, London W14 0NS, United Kingdom

www.sanctuarypublishing.com

Copyright: John Dutton, 2003

Music typesetting: Cambridge Notation

Cover image: Getty Images

All rights reserved. No part of this book may be reproduced in any form or by any electronic or mechanical means, including information storage or retrieval systems, without permission in writing from the publisher, except by a reviewer, who may quote brief passages.

While the publishers have made every reasonable effort to trace the copyright owners for any or all of the photographs in this book, there may be some omissions of credits, for which we apologise.

ISBN: 1-84492-005-4

100 Tips For Keyboards

You Should Have Been Told PART 1

John Dutton

smt

ACKNOWLEDGMENTS

Special thanks to: James Austin, Liz Walsh, Lynne Austin – Dutton, Pete Riley, Chris Francis, SMT (Alan Heal and Iain MacGregor), Norma Dutton, Levine Andrade, Neville Marten, Neil Robinson, Peter, Lawrence, Adam and Nathan for putting up with me, and Harry the cat for keeping me company.

To Bernard Dutton, a fine musician

BOOK CONTENTS

CD CONTENTS

Copyright: © John Dutton 2003 (this audio recording); © John Dutton 2003 (this instructional content).

CD voice-overs performed by Lynne Austin-Dutton.

'Released' copyright © John Dutton, 2002.

FOREWORD

Welcome to *100 Tips For Keyboards You Should Have Been Told*. You may well have a firm preconception of what this book could be like, so first of all I'm going to tell you what it's not. This is not a step-by-step tutorial book, even though I've covered a lot of the basic areas of playing and musicianship. You can buy plenty of books that show you every scale and chord under the sun or give you practical lessons in a long series of volumes.

Instead, this is a book designed to give you information which you can use to explore. The aim is to make the book as useful as possible, whether you have only the most basic understanding of keyboard playing or you've been making music for a while and are looking for something to help you fill in gaps you've skipped over. I know a lot of good players who have missed important areas of basic knowledge, so I'd urge you to take time and look at areas of the book which you may not initially feel are relevant. Everything I've done is designed to give you knowledge in areas that count. I might give you an example of something – a chord, for instance – but it's up to you to explore and discover the same chord in different keys and, most importantly, to relate that to your playing. Music is a very personal thing, so while trying to give you as many tools as possible, I also want to make you aware of how you can choose and adapt knowledge to suit your own style of playing.

Every exercise here has a meaning and a relevance – I won't take up your time leading you into endless chapters on theory which you can't connect with your music. However, some theory is useful to help you understand, as much as possible, why certain things happen. Although all of these pieces of information may take a while to click, things often suddenly slot into place in your mind. To do this, though, you've got to keep at it – worthwhile improvements can take time.

The later chapters of the book deal more with what happens in real-life scenarios – using and getting the most out of your equipment and handling different playing situations. Making full use of whatever gear you've got can transform your expectations and enjoyment of music. So even though you may tread the waters of modern technology a bit uneasily, it really is pretty simple to hook up a keyboard to a computer, for instance, and start making your own music. If you want to know how to set up your equipment to rehearse, or record, this information is relevant as well.

I'm a firm believer in all knowledge being useful – the more you know about something, the more enjoyment you get out of it. Music is music – enjoy it all.

John Dutton
Essex, May 2003

1 POSTURE

First reaction: skip this chapter. Right? After all, what has posture really got to do with playing, when it comes down to it? Either you can play or you can't.

Well, posture has quite a lot to do with playing, actually. In fact, a hell of a lot. However, what I won't do is get you hung up on the subject and give you so many instructions that playing is the last thing on your mind. What I want to do is to make you think, and to apply that thought in such a way that it becomes second nature. After a while you'll realise that it doesn't only benefit your playing, it makes you enjoy it more. And that's what counts, period.

Sitting Or Standing?

You may prefer (or be required) to stand and play on-stage. It usually looks more dynamic and may well improve your chances of pulling at the gig. However, I sometimes think that the only reason keyboard players stand on-stage is because they can. A drummer couldn't play effectively standing up (although Keith Moon had a good go sometimes!), and likewise for a keyboard player, in terms of ideal playing positions, sitting is better.

I'm not going to ignore the needs of players who stand – in fact, they well may be in more need of help. Firstly, though, I shall concentrate on the sitting position because that's where most of your playing time will be spent, whether practising or recording.

The Youth Of Today

Question: Can you remember how many times you were told to sit up straight at school? And when you went home you probably slouched in front of the TV as well...

Over the years, it's easy to get into a habit of sitting in a certain way, and it could be responsible for problems in everyday life. When you sit (or stand) in a static position for any length of time, you become much more aware of the effects of bad posture. If you drive, for instance, you'll know that, after a few hours at the wheel in some cars, backache creeps in, and it can get very uncomfortable

indeed, often due to a lack of support in the seat or a poor driving position.

When you play your keyboard, you don't want to be bothered by backache – a poor position will also compromise your playing ability. The habits I described above can lead to you setting up your gear to work around the situation, which won't help you in time. Believe me, I know a lot of musicians – not necessarily just keyboard players, either – who have had problems relating to the way in which they stand at, sit at or hold their instruments. Sometimes, it unfortunately takes something dramatic to make people change their ways. However, I don't want you to have to do it the hard way and have problems with posture limit your enjoyment of the music. That's the last thing you want. So, without getting into intricate detail, let's bear in mind a few factors that will hopefully help you play in a comfortable way and give you a good technical base to work from.

Sitting Down

An acoustic piano's keyboard is usually around 28 inches/71cm off the ground. If you own an electric piano resting on a tailor-made stand, the chances are it will be roughly the same height, as will a typical X-frame stand for a synth at its lowest position. I'd make this your starting point.

Next, use a chair (without arms) or stool that has a decent depth to the seat. The idea is not to sit right back onto it but towards the front end so that the weight of your body is firmly on your bottom. The seat must also be flat and firm – don't waste time with something that's soft or sinks in the middle.

When you sit down to play, think about the angle of your back – it should be running straight from the head down to the bottom. Let the weight sink onto your bottom, but not at the expense of arching your back. Your feet should be able to reach the floor comfortably, with the heels lightly taking a natural amount of weight. If you use a sustain pedal, this is especially important, as the heel is used as a pivot for the rest of the foot to depress and release the pedal.

Many people play while sitting (or standing) too high. Perching too high will encourage you to slouch and arch your back, which can lead to a whole range of problems. Accompanying this is a resultant tendency to drop the head to look down at the keyboard or read music. This really is bad news. If it's a habit you have, try to get out of it as soon as possible. Don't forget that your eyes are designed to move in your head – if you let them do the work, there's usually no need to angle your head down. If you haven't got one, buy a decent stool at a good height and get used to it, so that you play in the same position wherever you go.

Now, all of this may give you the impression that you sit at the keyboard dead still, fearful of moving a muscle in case you move to the wrong position. This is emphatically not the case. If you move around a lot when you play, that's fine. Instead, regard the advice above as general information to store and use if it works for you.

Standing

Playing standing up brings its own set of issues. Unless (or even if) an X-frame stand is set really high, you're likely to end up crouched over the keyboard with your head bent down – as we've seen, not good. An A-frame or other vertical-bar stand is a common choice, particularly if you're using more than one keyboard. That's OK, although you may need to reappraise how high the keyboard actually has to be, remembering that the same things apply as when sitting down. It's no use having a keyboard set at waist height and expecting to be able to play anything. People do, but it's

unnecessary, it's uncomfortable and it severely limits playing ability. Instead, try having the keyboard much nearer chest height so you can adopt a more natural position. Don't use the keyboard to lean on, either – stand up with your back as straight as possible and play the instrument without using it to prop yourself up. (A note of caution: if you are putting a single keyboard higher than usual, be careful that the stand doesn't become top-heavy and crash to the ground.)

When using a sustain pedal while sitting, body weight rests on the bottom and the heel is used as a pivot, as described above. However, when standing up, your feet are used to take the weight of your body and also balance it. This means that you need to bring the pedal closer than usual or you'll adopt an extremely awkward position with the pedal too far underneath the keyboard. A good idea is to gaffer-tape the pedal in position on-stage so it doesn't move. This can still be a bit awkward, as you partially lose balance when weight gets taken off the toes, and if this is noticeable you should make sure that the backs of your knees aren't locked tight, sagging them slightly to help you balance.

As we explore basic playing technique, the benefits of good playing posture will become more apparent. In time you'll regard it almost as a good friend, as you'll be relaxed and it will help to advance your playing more than you realise.

If you're interested in learning more about posture, it could be worthwhile checking out the Alexander technique, which is used by many musicians and actors to help them to relax and perform to their maximum on-stage. Contact details can be found easily on the Internet.

2 BASIC TECHNIQUE

'One cannot begin at the end.' Frederick Chopin

Technique – another subject that's often misunderstood. On hearing someone perform a flashy run, it's natural to remark, 'Oh, what a wonderful technique.' That's missing the point, really. It's not just what the player is doing in terms of making the sound, it depends on how he or she is achieving it. The player in question might not necessarily have a good technique at all; he or she might just be comfortable with that particular run, or holding tension, adopting bad habits and so on in order to be able to do it. Technique goes far, far deeper than appearing to be able to execute a quick run or something similarly flashy – it's something that is at the very core of your playing. Providing you keep up your facility on the instrument, you should never lose it, only improve.

We've looked briefly at how posture and the way you sit or stand at the keyboard has an important effect on playing. That is perhaps the most basic form of technique in itself – it's allowing you to have the base to work from in order to progress. The best explanation I have for describing technique, and what it means to your playing, is that it's your body's ability to do any task that your mind sets it in as efficiently and effortlessly as possible. It doesn't require a great deal of effort to play a keyboard, any more than a boxer with a knockout punch hits particularly hard. Instead, it's all about finding the important elements and getting them working in an effective – yet simple – way.

Technical ability can be measured at different levels. The important thing is that firstly you become comfortable within the musical area you're in now, be it beginner or more advanced. There is actually nothing wrong with having a simple yet effective technique, depending on the kind of music you want to play – it's far better to play something simple properly than to try to clatter through a more complicated part and never get it right. Of course, I really want you to set your goals as high as possible, but this should never be at the expense of getting your form right.

Getting Your Form Right

Sit down at the keyboard as near to the middle as possible, close enough to allow the fingers to reach well towards the backs of the keys. Now put your hands on the keyboard. The elbows should naturally push outwards slightly – certainly don't make an effort to hold them in against the body. The wrist should be relaxed and straight with the forearm – don't allow it to drop or push up. Bend the fingers so that the tips are in contact with the keyboard and slightly bent. The hand should now create an arch. In the past, an old favourite among piano teachers was to allow a pencil to be put through the arch underneath the hand. This can encourage a wrist position that's slightly too high, but it's a useful starting point to gauge basic hand position. Long fingernails make it difficult to keep the fingers bent – the little pad at the top of your finger should be the part that makes contact with the keys. If you can hear your fingernails clattering, it's best to get them cut, I'm afraid.

Just sit and think how things feel for a moment. It's quite common for wrists to hold quite a bit of tension. Without allowing them to drop down, consciously allow them to relax as much as possible. When you do this, you may become aware of a little more weight falling onto the fingertips. That's good. Hold the position without playing for a few seconds and remember the feeling.

We need to now perform some simple exercises to help get this form we've created into our minds. These particular exercises are based around *scales* and *arpeggios* – the nuts and bolts of music.

With each exercise and piece of music that follows, there will be a reference to fingering in the form of numbers from 1–5. To avoid any doubt, 1 indicates thumb, 5 indicates little finger and 2, 3 and 4 represent the fingers in between.

Keyboard Orientation

When I said to sit as near to the middle of the keyboard as possible, that's for a few reasons (some which are pretty obvious). Obviously, it means that you can reach to the

▲ Track 1

▲ Track 2

extreme right or left of the keyboard with the relevant hand, and therefore cover all of the available notes. It also means (in the context of a piano keyboard, at least) that you're sitting near to a note called *middle C*. Middle C is perhaps the most relevant point of reference you can have on a piano-type keyboard. While it is not a dividing line, as such, between the areas that the right and left hands play in, you're likely to play more with your right hand in the area from middle C upwards (higher) than your left, and conversely in the area downwards from middle C (lower) more with your left than your right.

There is a possible complication with this on an electronic keyboard. A piano usually comes with an 88-note keyboard (full length) and is not transposable. Middle C is therefore always in the same physical position on the keyboard, between the two pedals. A synthesiser may have a much shorter keyboard and a C in the middle of the keyboard may not be at the same pitch as that on a piano. In other words, it could be playing a higher (or lower) C. On most keyboards, this can be changed easily. So, using the CD and with this in mind, we're going to check where middle C is on your keyboard. You can alter its position if necessary. Check out the diagrams opposite.

If middle C is not in the centre of your keyboard for whatever reason and you can't change its position, just play the C in physically the most central point on your keyboard for the purposes of this exercise.

Playing A Basic Exercise

Put your right hand onto the keyboard as described in the section above and place your thumb on middle C. The centre joint of the thumb should have a slight bend outwards. Now place the other fingers onto each subsequent white note, travelling up the keyboard – D, E, F, G. Remember to keep that arch formed with your hand. Now, while keeping that arched hand position intact and making sure your wrist is relaxed, lift your thumb up slightly and depress it to sound the note of middle C. While you're doing this, keep the other fingers resting lightly on or as close to the keyboard as possible – you may find this difficult initially, but it will become easier with time.

Bring up the thumb to release the note and at the same time lift up and depress the second finger to play the next note so that, as one is released, the next is played. There should be no audible gap between the two notes – but no overlap, either. This style of playing is called *legato*, an Italian word meaning 'smoothly'. Continue along with the sequence in this legato manner until you've played G with your little finger, then play the notes back down again to middle C.

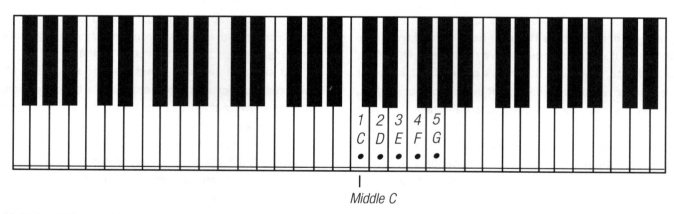

Right-hand five-note exercise

Let's play the left hand on its own. Place your little finger on the next C down, an *octave* beneath middle C, and the other four fingers on each following white note, just as you did with the right hand. Follow the same procedure to play legato-fashion up to the G and back down again, making sure the wrist is relaxed and the hand remains arched.

Repeat this with both hands separately a few times, remembering how it feels, and then try both hands together.

This exercise should be played slowly – listen to the CD for an example of how it should sound. Try to reach the bottom of each note – don't skate on the tops of the notes so that they don't fully sound.

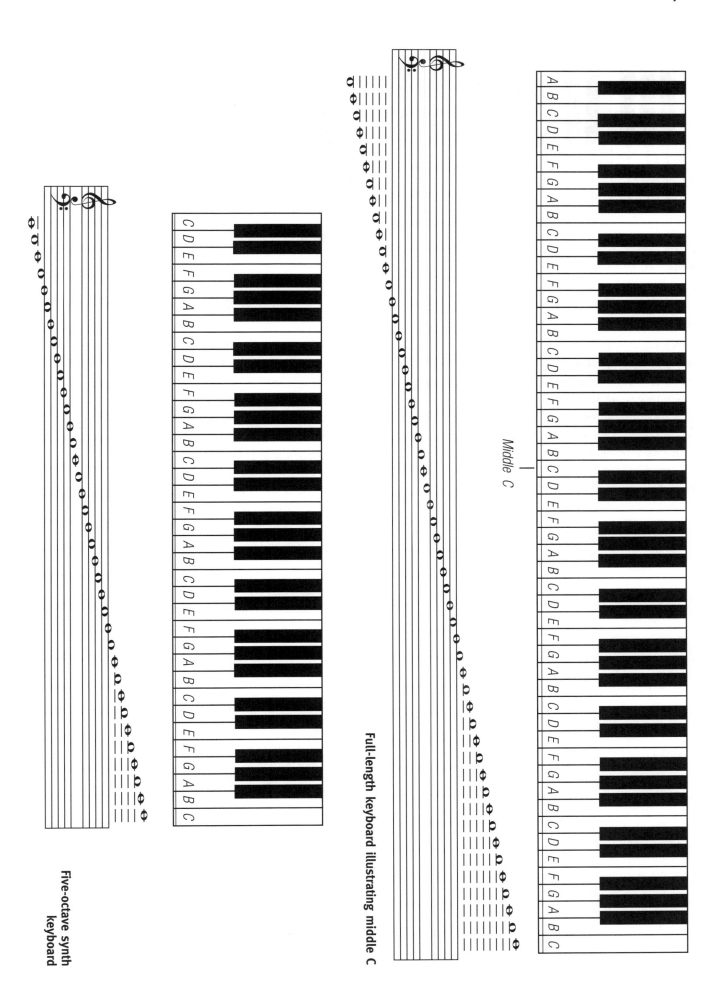

Full-length keyboard illustrating middle C

Five-octave synth keyboard

Middle C

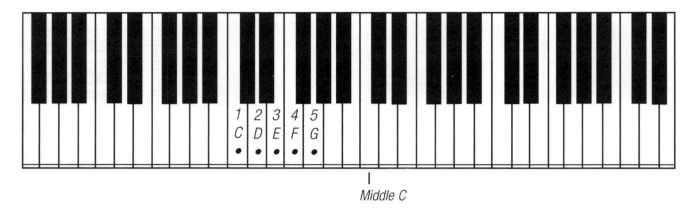

Middle C

Left-hand five-note exercise

This exercise may be basic, but it's also extremely valuable. Irrespective of your playing level, it's always useful to sit down for a few minutes and pay attention to posture and basic technique like this. In this way, when you're in a playing or performing situation, you'll find that your body has retained a lot of this physical information and you won't have to be aware of it as much. It will really help, though, if you do this for at least a few minutes every day – especially at first – in order to get used to your playing position and these basic aspects of playing technique. I'm not going to bang on about practice levels and the like at this stage of the book, but you will feel the results if you do something like this every day. Little and often is a good approach.

3 BASIC EXERCISES

'All I really need to know I learned in kindergarten.' *Robert Fulgham*

So far we've looked at how valuable basic posture and technique are. But when are we actually going to play something and apply this musically?

Well, the exercise we did in the last chapter is a more relevant musical exercise than you might think. Indeed, all rudimentary exercises such as scales and arpeggios are, and that's the way you should think of them. Sometimes this is not apparent straight away, so to give you an example before we move on, I'm going to show you a basic chord born out of that last exercise.

Place both of your hands on the keyboard in the same position as for the previous exercise. We played five notes in a row, from C to G, with both hands, each note played separately. I'm going to show you how to play a major chord without having to change your hand position. Let's take the right hand on its own first. Instead of playing the sequence from C to G in separate notes as before, locate the position of your thumb, third and fifth fingers, which should be resting (but not playing) the notes of C, E and G respectively. Then I want you to lift up the hand – with a relaxed wrist, of course – and play those three notes at the same time. When you lift up the hand, you may raise the wrist slightly, allowing it to return to its normal angle – parallel to the floor – once the chord has sounded.

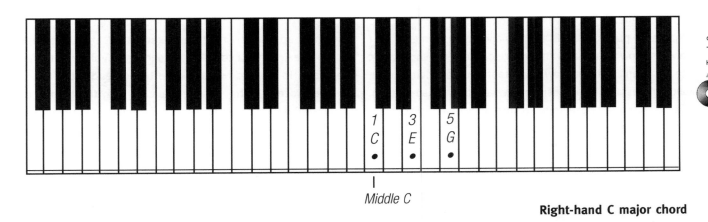

Middle C

Right-hand C major chord

▶ Track 3

The dots mark the notes you should play, with middle C marked so you can orientate yourself on the keyboard. The fingering is indicated above the respective note name.

With your left hand, locate the notes of C and G only with your fifth finger and thumb in the same position as the last exercise, then lift up the hand with a relaxed wrist and play those two notes at the same time.

For maximum effect, both hands should be played together. Make sure that each finger reaches the bottom of its respective note to ensure that it sounds properly.

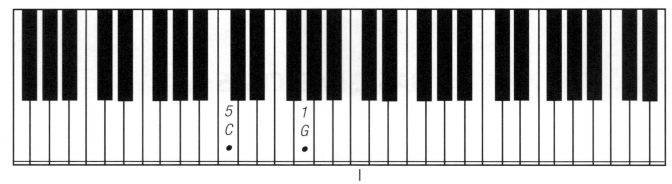

Left-hand C major chord (fifth interval only)   *Middle C*

This arrangement of notes is also called a C major *triad* (three notes). Thousands of well-known songs start with this chord – think of John Lennon's 'Imagine' or Oasis's 'Don't Look Back In Anger', to name a couple.

Why don't you play three notes in the left hand as well as the right? Well, you can try playing the E with your third finger as well to mirror what you do with your right hand, but I think you'll agree that, when you play both hands together, it sounds tighter and cleaner with only those two notes sounding in the left hand. We'll cover voicings such as this, and why they matter, in a later chapter.

You can see that these exercises will have some direct bearing on things you're likely to end up playing. That's how I'd like you to think of them, as well as using them to hone your basic technique, because playing an instrument is about making music, after all.

Major Scales

You may already know what a major scale is. However, I find that many pupils, even if they play another instrument, don't always know what scales and arpeggios are. More importantly, they haven't realised how important it is for their playing and understanding of music to have a proper grasp of them. So, even though we're going to start off with a basic C major scale, I'd urge you to follow this through (it won't take long), as scales are also excellent for warming up.

The five-note exercise we've already performed comprises just over half of a C major scale. We're now going to learn all of it.

Right hand only first. Find the same hand position you performed the previous exercise in, with your thumb on middle C and your other fingers resting lightly over the next four notes, up to G. Now play the first three notes – C, D and E – with thumb, second and third finger as before. After you've played the E, however, instead of playing F with the fourth finger, tuck your thumb under the arch of the hand to play the F. It's normal for beginners to find the wrist and forearm pushing out at an angle to help this happen – it can be a bit awkward at first. As much as you can, though, keep your hand in the same arched position and keep the sound legato, as you did in the previous exercise, trying to play that F with the thumb at the same time as releasing the previous note.

Once the thumb is on the F, you'll see that you can play the next four notes without having to change hand position again, up to where the little finger plays C an octave above middle C. That's a complete ascending (ie going up) C major scale. To come down again (ie to descend), just reverse the process – after having played F with the thumb, put the third finger over to the E and follow down to middle C with your second finger and thumb. That transition with the thumb is a bit easier coming down.

Track 4

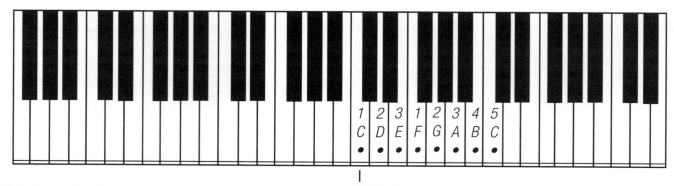

Right-hand C major scale   *Middle C*

Next, the left hand. Again, start on the C an octave down from middle C with your fifth finger on the C. When you've reached the G with your thumb, move your third finger over the top to play the A and use your second finger and thumb on the B and C respectively. Coming down is again a reverse process (although you may find it a little more awkward coming down, as the thumb has to be tucked under to play the G).

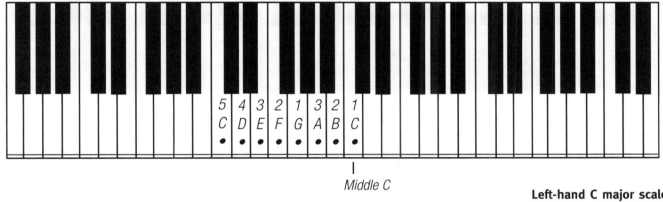

Middle C

Left-hand C major scale

Now it's time for the logical conclusion to these exercises – both hands together. Again, find the starting position with both hands on the keyboard. As you've seen when playing both hands individually, the hand positions change at different points. When ascending the keyboard, the right-hand thumb tucks under for the F and the left-hand third finger goes over for the A. Coming back down the scale, the order is reversed, with the left-hand thumb now going under for the G and the right-hand third finger crossing over for the E. Some people grasp this more quickly than others, but if it takes a little practice, stick at it because it's an invaluable sequence to learn. The same fingering is used for many major and minor scales and will help greatly when you need to perform quick runs and other, more advanced, passages.

Major Arpeggios

Arpeggios are exercises like scales, but they are formed around the structures of chords. Remember the C major chord you just played? Well, you can see that the chord is formed by taking the first, third and fifth notes of the C major scale – C, E and G. Well, a C major arpeggio is based around just these three notes, plus another C at the octave above. Taking the right hand first, it looks like this:

Track 5

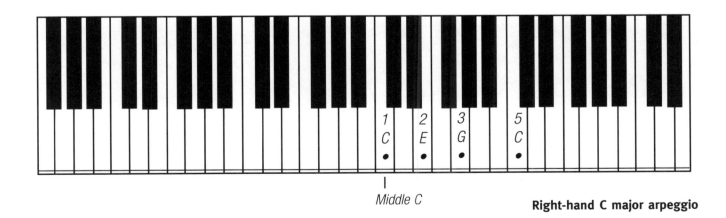

Middle C

Right-hand C major arpeggio

Try to keep your hand in the same position when you play this arpeggio – make sure the wrist is relaxed and don't let it rotate noticeably, although a certain amount of movement is OK.

The left-hand part turns up like this:

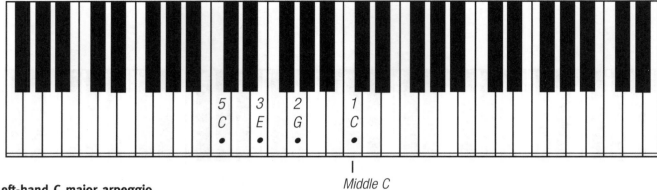

Left-hand C major arpeggio

Middle C

When you're comfortable with each hand individually, perform the exercise with both hands together. It's often easier than a scale, as there's no thumb to tuck under at the moment. Remember to treat these exercises not as a chore but as a valuable tool for warming up and improving your general dexterity.

4 STARTING TO READ MUSIC

'Life is like music: it can be composed by ear, feeling and instinct, not only by rule.' Samuel Barber

What is a stave? Well, it's where we start to explore a major area of musical knowledge: reading music from a page.

In my opinion, reading music is of enormous benefit. Lots of very fine professional players don't read, instead relying on their hearing of music (playing by ear) as their main tool. However, many of them honestly wish that they *did* read music but consider it too late to be able to relate it to their playing. Certainly, to have a good musical ear – to be able to identify chords and interpret music without having it written down – is extremely important, but it shouldn't be an either/or situation. The most beneficial way of learning to read music is at the same time as you develop your playing and hearing skills, so that you can think of them all as one. There are sometimes negative prejudices surrounding musicians who read, usually held by those who can't. Forget them. Providing you use it in the right way – as a complement to your playing – an ability to read music can only be to your advantage. The fewer gaps you have in your understanding of music, the more you'll get out of it. Guaranteed.

Music is written down on *staves*, which are groups of five horizontal lines linked together. If you look at a typical piece of keyboard music, it will have two staves placed together. The top one is for the right hand, the lower for the left. Each stave (or staff) has five lines and will have a symbol such as 𝄞 (treble clef) or 𝄢 (bass clef) at the start. When you see a treble clef, it usually relates to the right hand; the bass clef refers to the left. Hence usually the treble clef will be at the start of the top, right-hand stave, and the bass clef will be at the start of the bottom, left-hand stave. There are exceptions, but we'll come to those later.

Taking the treble clef first, I'll show you how what we've already done is written down. Firstly, let's see what middle C looks like:

The right-hand part of the scale of C major, which you've already played, looks like this:

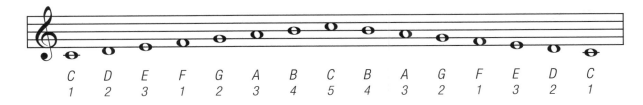

C major scale ascending and descending in treble clef with annotated notes and fingering

Here's middle C on the bass-clef stave along with the left-hand part of C major scale:

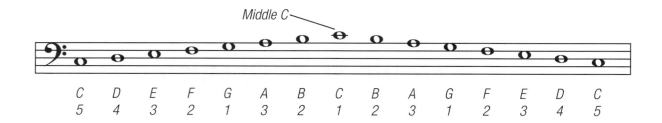

Both hands together, therefore, looks like this:

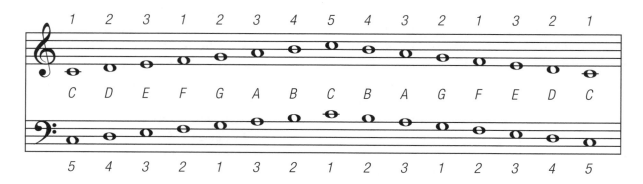

**C major scale, ascending and descending,
in treble and bass clefs**

The C major chord we played looks like this:

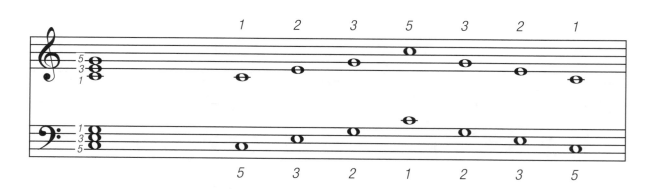

C major root-position chord and arpeggio

It's pretty easy to see how notes on the stave relate to the keyboard. This scale, as written, relates only to a certain area on the stave. The diagram below gives a more comprehensive guide:

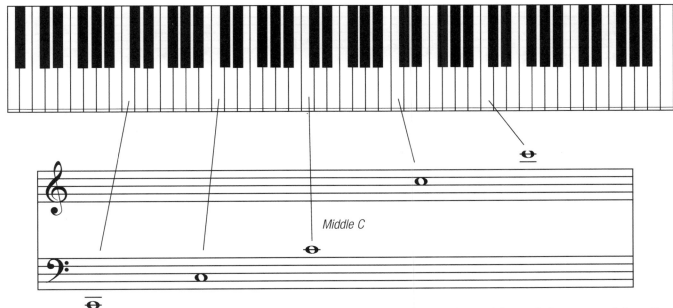

Middle C

A wider range of notes on treble- and bass-clef staves and how they relate to their positions on the keyboard (88-note, full-length version)

Looks pretty straightforward? It is. It takes time, though, before you know instinctively how the notes on a stave relate to their positions on a keyboard. My priority is to get you playing something as quickly as possible, understanding what you're doing on the way. This is best done by playing pieces of music, so I'm going to press on with that in mind. In order to do this, we need to touch on a couple of subjects: keys and rhythm.

Keys And Harmonic Structures

When you played that scale, you played all seven notes in the key of C major. Therefore, all those notes – C, D, E, F, G, A and B – can be said to be in the key of *C major*. The key note in a scale (in this case, C) is also known as the *tonic*.

If you were to count all of the notes, white and black, within an octave – for instance, between the two C notes in the scale – you would find 12, not 7. However, each scale, major or minor, is made up from a certain pattern that uses only seven different notes from within this 12-note selection.

Therefore, not all of the notes in a scale are right next to each other. The gap between two notes that are adjacent to each other is called a *semitone*. Looking at the diagram above, you can see that E to F is a semitone, as is B to C.

C to D, though, has a (black) note in between, and the gap (or *interval*) between them is known as a *tone*. Any scale, be it major or minor, is made up of a pattern of *semitones* (also called *halftones*) and tones.

Major scales just happen to have the following order of tones and semitones: tonic (key note), tone, tone, semitone, tone, tone, tone, semitone, tonic. That's what gives them the sound they have.

Each of the 12 notes within an octave has its own scales and key structure. C major is a straightforward choice to start with as it (uniquely) uses only white notes and is easy to remember. For reasons that will become clear, new major keys are covered in a certain order, starting with G.

With your right hand, start on G and use the same fingering as with C major. Follow the white notes up and when you get to F, the last note before you reach the G at the top of the scale, see how it sounds. Your ear may well tell you that something is not quite right somewhere...

Remember what I said about the major scale being made up of a pattern of steps – tone, tone, semitone, tone, tone, tone, semitone? Well, while following that pattern has got us up to F using just white notes, the F itself just doesn't sound right. If you look at the interval between the last two notes (semitone), you have your answer – F isn't right next to G, is it? But the black note in between *is*, and it's called F sharp. Therefore the seventh note of G major scale is F sharp, and F sharp is the key signature of G major.

If you saw this written down, it would be even more apparent. If a note is to be played as a sharp, it is indicated by a sign – ♯ – and G major appears on a stave like this:

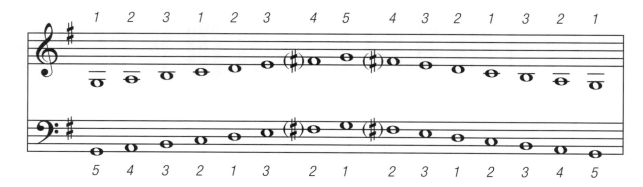

G major scale

I've put the key signature for this scale and all subsequent ones at the start of the staves in front of the scale, which is where you'd expect to see it at the start of a piece of music. Normally when this occurs there would then be no subsequent ♯ sign in front of the note when written, so I've

put it in brackets to remind you.

As with C major, try the left hand on its own next and then both hands together when you're confident you can do it. When you've got this under your belt, try the G major arpeggio and chord:

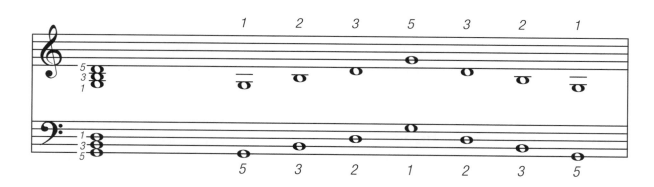

G major chord and arpeggio

As we're getting through this pretty quickly, the next major key we need to get to know is D major. Whereas G major had one sharp, D major has two. We keep the sharp we've already encountered – F♯ – and we add another. There's a very easy way of finding out what it is...

You'll remember that the last interval before the tonic

is reached (between the seventh and eighth notes) is a semitone. That's why G major has an F♯ – it's a semitone below G. So now that we're in the key of D, which has got two sharps, we know already that it's going to have an F sharp in it. (You can confirm that by following through the tone, tone, semitone, tone, tone, semitone pattern.) We

▲ Track 6

know there's a semitone gap between the seventh and eighth notes, so as the eighth note is D, the seventh one

must be C♯, the black note directly below D. (The new note to be sharpened in major keys is always the seventh note.)

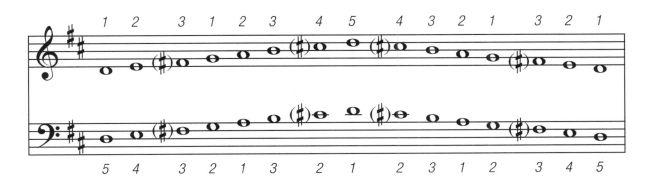

▲ Track 7

D major scale

So, we know three major chords and three major scales: C, G and D.

As we're marching through this, we'll cover another couple of major chords: A, which has three sharps; and E,

which has four. Taking A first, we already know that it has F♯ and C♯ already in its key signature. To find the new sharp in a major key, we go to the seventh note – in this case, G – and sharpen it. The A major triad looks like this:

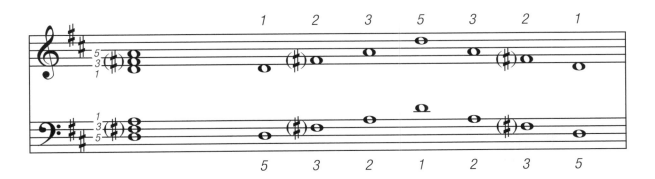

D major chord and arpeggio

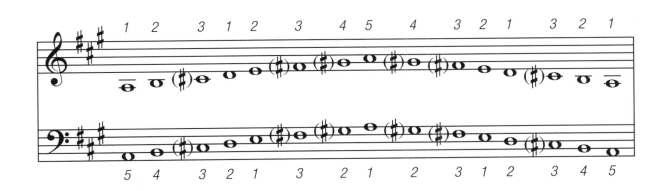

▲ Track 8

A major scale

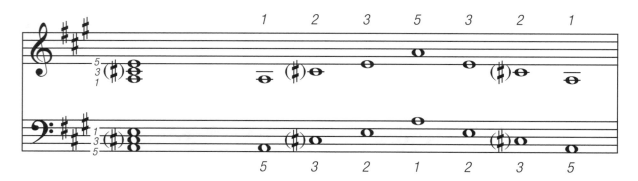

A major chord and arpeggio

Likewise, we know that E major will have F#, C# and G# already in its key signature, and to find the new sharp we again go to the seventh note – D – and sharpen that. Have a look below:

▲ Track 9

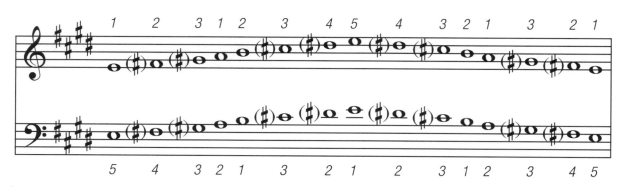

E major scale

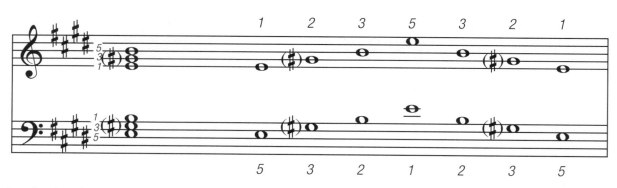

E major chord and arpeggio

So now we've got five major chords under our belt – we know the key signatures for each of them and also what they look like on paper. I could have told you the information a bit more quickly than that, but I wanted you to understand it, hear it and see it all as much as possible – no gaps, remember?

We're getting close to playing along with a track on the CD, but first let's look at a few elements of rhythm.

5 BASIC RHYTHM

'Rhythm lies at the heart of play.' *Alan Watts, philosopher*

Rhythm governs our lives. Our hearts beat, keeping us alive, and our bodies naturally respond to external sources of rhythm. Worked around this is the rhythmic structure of music, which in the case of popular music, in particular, is often designed to get your foot tapping, get you jigging along, whatever. It's based around a *pulse*, or a *beat*, the speed of which determines the nature of the track. A good example of a beat is the solid bass-drum part of a typical dance record. It's that constant, relentless thud – often heard through your neighbour's wall or from the open window of a passing car – that drives the track along. What that kind of bass drum part is usually doing is playing along with the pulse of the track, usually in the case of an up-tempo (quick) dance record at about 140bpm (beats per minute). That's quite fast – enough to get you knackered after dancing along for a few numbers! A slower track, such as a ballad, could typically be anywhere from

70–100 beats per minute. In the case of a ballad, you wouldn't have such an audible example as that constant bass drum banging through from start to end, but it would still have a pulse that can be felt running through it.

However, a piece of music has to have a rhythmic structure – a basic framework – within which this pulse, or *beat*, can be placed. Depending on the type of piece, the emphasis, or *feel*, of the beat can also be different. 'Happy Birthday' doesn't feel the same as 'Land Of Hope And Glory', does it?

So we divide these beats up into bars. At extremes, a bar may last anything from 2 to 15 beats, although popular music – including our mythical dance-track example – very often has four beats to the bar. This is known commonly as being 'in four' or 'in four-four' (written 4/4). The number of beats a bar has denotes its *time signature*.

A time signature is represented on a stave as follows:

4/4 time signature

Track 10

Within a bar of music, we need to have a means of explaining when notes should be played and for how long they should last. For a simple example, the bass-drum part described above was being played on every beat, therefore

being played four times in a bar. Now, imagine that you wanted to play along with that bass-drum part – say, on middle C – so that what you played sounded at exactly the same time. It would look like this:

Bar of quarter notes (or crotchets) on middle C

Each of these dots on the stave represents a beat. The *crotchet* signs (♩) indicate that the note is one beat long. If you wanted to make each note last twice as long, for two beats, it would be written as a *minim*, like this: ♩

A two-bar example of minims would look like this (I've also played it through on the CD):

Two-bar example of minims (half notes)

If you wanted a note to last for four beats, you'd use a *semibreve*, which looks like this: o

A four-bar example of semibreves would look like this (again, I've played it through on the CD):

Four-bar example of semibreves (whole notes)

So we're going to have a go at playing a simple track along with the CD. The tempo of the track is 80 beats per minute (marked at the top of the score), which feels quite slow and easy.

Track 11

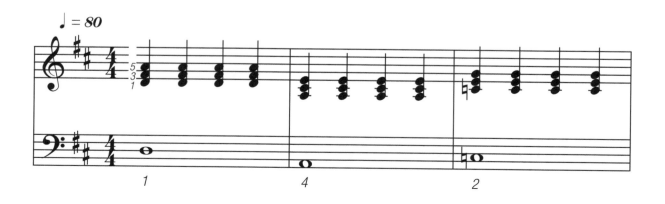

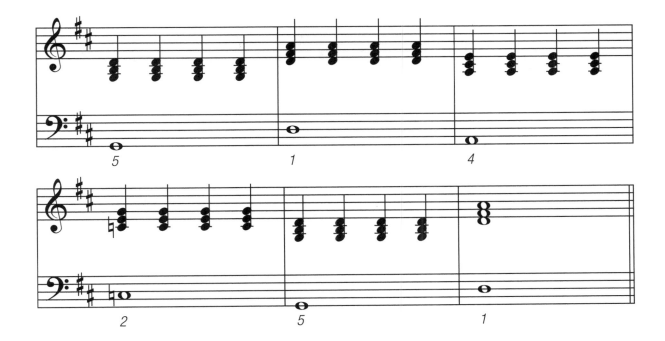

This track uses four of the chords we've encountered in the book – D, A, C and G major. The piece is in D major, so it has two sharps written in at the start of each stave to remind you of the key signature. This means that any F or C sharps within the following bars don't have to be marked with a ♯ sign. If, for instance, in bars 3 and 7, a C♯ is not to be played (we're playing a C major chord, so that makes sense) a little natural sign (♮) is inserted in front of the relevant note (or notes) indicating that it should be played as a normal, unsharpened C. Once this sign has appeared in front of a note (in this case the C), each subsequent C within that bar is also to be played as a C natural.

At the end of the piece, instead of another line indicating the end of the bar, you will see two bar lines. This is called a *double bar*, and it always indicates the end of a piece.

Let's look at the right hand on its own first. As you can see, the piece is in 4/4 and the chords in the right-hand part are all to be played along with the pulse of the track. Use the same fingering – thumb and third and fifth fingers – for each of the chords.

The left-hand part is even more simple: only one note per bar, each lasting for four beats. The fingering is designed so that the hand can stay in the same basic position – it should feel easy to play.

When you're comfortable with playing each hand individually, try both hands together.

There is another note value we should understand before moving on. Called either a *quaver* or an *eighth note*, it is half the length of a crotchet (or quarter note). Therefore, two of them make up a beat, and eight of them make up a bar in 4/4. Written singly, they look like this ♪, and if two or more are played one after the other, they are grouped together, as follows:

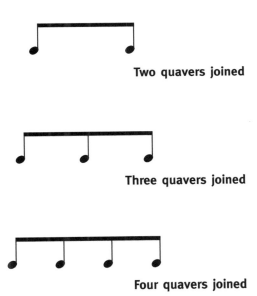

Two quavers joined

Three quavers joined

Four quavers joined

A bar of quavers played on a single note, as shown above, can be heard on the CD.

As a simple exercise, I've written down four tunes in different rhythms over the page. You can refer to them on the CD to hear how they should sound, or you can have a go at them yourself first of all.

Track 12

1 2 3 5   1 2 3 5   3   4   1

1   5   3   1   2   4 5   4

5 5 2   3 3 1   2 3 5 3   2

1   5   4 3 2   3 1 5 4   3

More About Time Signatures, Note Values And Rests

▲ Track 13

Time signatures can be broken down into two distinct types: *simple* and *compound*. Don't worry if this is starting to sound a little complex, because it really isn't! The 4/4 time signature illustrated above is a simple type. The first figure (4) denotes the number of beats in the bar. The second figure (in this case also a 4) refers to the length of beat. When the second figure is 4, it means that the length of a beat is measured as a crotchet, or quarter note.

I mentioned a little while ago about how the emphasis, or feel, of a beat can be different, depending on the type of piece. The 4/4 time signature is very commonly used because it 'feels' easy to listen and play along to. Imagine that dance beat thumping along, and you can count – and feel – the pulse of 4 running through each bar.

Other time signatures, however, can also give music a very distinctive sound, and we'll look at a few of those now.

One time signature that you're likely to audibly recognise is 3/4. Simply, it means (looking at the 3, the first figure) that there are three beats in a bar, with each beat (looking at the 4, the second figure) lasting for a crotchet, or quarter note. The most famous types of pieces in 3/4 time signatures are waltzes, such as 'The Blue Danube'. The English National Anthem and 'Happy Birthday' are other well-known pieces in 3/4. These may be slightly uncool examples, but they illustrate the feel of 3/4 very well.

With familiarity, you can tell 3/4 and 4/4 apart quite easily, such are their different feels. Particularly with 3/4, the slight emphasis on the first beat is helpful when it comes to finding the start of the bar. Try counting out loud along to each time signature – it will help you to recognise them more quickly when you hear them.

We should touch on a time signature in compound time before leaving this section. Compound time sounds a lot more complicated than it actually is – it's only another type of time signature. There is more than one compound time signature, but the only one that we're concerned with right now is 6/8. Thinking back to the explanations behind 4/4 or 3/4 time, we looked at the first number (giving the number of beats in a bar) and the second number (telling us for how long each beat lasts) in turn. Every time signature in the musical world is worked out in this way. So, with 6/8, we know that there are six beats in a bar. The eight refers to the length of each beat, and means eighth notes, or quavers – six beats, each lasting for one quaver.

Why not just have six crotchet (quarter-note) beats in a bar? Well, this time signature is measured in eighth notes to reflect the feel and emphasis of particular pieces. What's more, if it was measured in quarter notes, it would make the tempo very fast. We move into compound time (anything over eight – with an eighth-note pulse – is classed as being in compound time) and measure the pulse in eighth notes for those reasons. But the best way to explain how 6/8 works is to hear it.

Written down, it looks like this:

A simple 6/8 tune

You may recognise the characteristic sound of 6/8 in many well-known pop songs, often slower numbers. Also, you can see that the six quavers are divided up into two groups of three. While together they make up six quavers, these two groups give an emphasis of two in the bar, rather than six.

Rests

Music is obviously not just one long, continuous stream of sound; it has space and periods of silence known as rests. Rests are simply indications of areas in a part or piece of music where the composer wants you to stop playing for a defined period. For each of the note values we've learnt so far, there is a rest of an equivalent length – eighth note, quarter note, half note and full note. (There are also shorter notes and variations of existing notes yet to learn.)

The diagrams below show what each of these looks like when written down:

Eighth note and rest   *Quarter note and rest*   *Half note and rest*   *Full note and rest*

Note values and corresponding rests

The tunes below – one in 4/4 and one in 3/4 – feature all of these rests:

Short tune in 4/4 with rests

Short tune with rests in 3/4

An important and common variation is the use of dotted notes and rests. These are very simple to understand. A dot written after a note, as illustrated below, means that the note value is now half as long again. In other words, referring to this half note, which had a value of two beats, it now has three:

A dotted quarter note or rest has a length of one and a half beats:

A dotted eighth note or rest has a length of three-quarters of a beat:

There are many more forms of note values and rhythms in music, many of which give very definite characteristics to its sound – such as in Latin music, for instance. However, a good grasp of these basics will set you on a long way; everything you learn here can be used as building blocks in the future.

At this stage, we've covered only the very basics and there's lots more to explain, but we're close enough to be able to read and play a piece of music.

6 MAJOR AND MINOR CHORDS

'Do you know that our soul is composed of harmony?' Leonardo Da Vinci

We'll now have a brief look at further keys: major and minor. However, as I've explained, the purpose of this book is not to be a step-by-step tutorial; instead, I want to encourage you to think and find out a few things for yourself. What I want to do is give you an idea of how and why these things matter, and to have explained the basics so that you can apply the knowledge you've acquired to learn more. I've included a chart with key signatures of major and minor keys for reference at the back of the book, and, after having explained more of the basics about major and minor keys, I'm going to move on to other areas of playing.

More Major Chords

You may have noticed a progression when moving onto the next major key with sharp-based key signatures. For instance, we did C major first (no sharps). To get to the

next key, G major, go up the C major scale to the fifth note and you get to G. To find the next key from G, go to the fifth note in the scale, and you get to D.

This cycle or process carries on through to the other majors we've covered so far: A and E, and on to B and F♯ majors.

This has still left us with a few more keys to cover. Because of the structure of the 12-note scale, some keys need to have *flats* (indicated by a ♭ sign), rather than sharps, in their key signatures. An example is F major: it follows exactly the same major-scale pattern as before: (tonic) tone, tone, semitone, tone, tone, semitone, (tonic). So that makes the first four notes F, G, A and B♭. Why not A♯, you ask? Because each note in a scale has to have a different letter name – you can't have two 'A' notes – A and A♯, to cite this particular instance.

Track 15

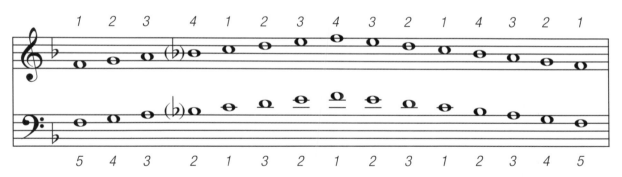

F major scale with fingering

F major chord with fingering

F major, therefore, has one flat in its key signature: B♭.

Major keys with flat key signatures also have different

fingering, and for this reason some people don't bother to learn them. However, it's not difficult and well worth the effort.

To find the next flat key, instead of going to the fifth note of the existing scale, as we did with the sharp-based keys, go to the fourth note instead. The new flat will then be the fourth note of that scale. In the case of F major, the fourth note is B♭. B♭ has two flats in its key signature: B♭ itself and its fourth note, E♭. E♭ major has three flats: B♭, E♭ and its fourth note, A♭ – you get the idea. This process can be followed through to each subsequent flat major key.

Minor Keys And Chords

So far, all of the chords, scales and arpeggios we've encountered have been majors. So what is a minor key?

Well, it's easy to show you, using chords as an example. To play a C major chord, take the first, third and fifth notes of the C major scale – C, E and G – and play them together. To change this to a minor chord, keep the C and G but, instead of playing the E, go one semitone down to the E♭:

▲ Track 16

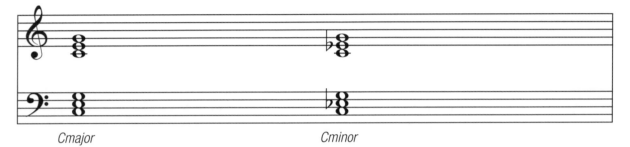

Cmajor   *Cminor*

You'll hear the difference between the two straight away. In corny music-lesson parlance, major chords are 'happy' and minor chords are 'sad.' There is some substance to this description as, in contrast to the major chord, the minor does have a more sombre sound. But it's the way in which they're used within music – taking factors such as tempo and phrasing into account – that often gives this impression.

Put simply, the difference between major and minor chords centres on the third note of the scale. A minor chord has what's called a *flattened third* – ie, the third note of the scale is a semitone lower (flatter) than its major counterpart. This is a rule that works with any key.

Minor Scales

A minor scale is similar in many ways to a major one. However, whereas a major scale has semitone gaps between notes 3–4 and 7–8, and follows the interval pattern (tonic), tone, tone, semitone, tone, tone, semitone, (tonic), a minor scale follows a slightly different pattern. We already know that it has a flattened third, so the opening two intervals will be (tonic), tone, semitone. What happens afterwards depends on the type of minor scale you're playing. We'll deal here with the natural (or pure) minor scale.

We'll start with the key of A minor as it shares the same key signature as C major.

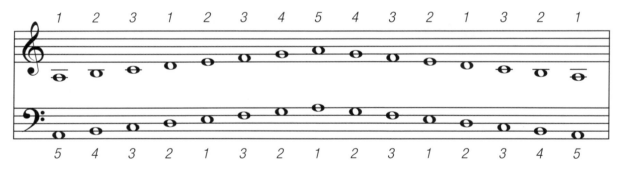

Pure A minor scale with fingering

When a major and minor key share the same key signature, they are said to be *relative* to each other, so A minor is the *relative minor* to C major. To find the relative minor key from a major, follow the scale of the major key up to the sixth degree to find the tonic of its relative minor. This process can be followed through every key, so once you know the key signature of a major key, its relative minor is easily found. To find the relative major key from a minor, follow the minor scale up to its third note.

Using this method, you can very easily find the minor key that has one sharp – for instance, go to G major and go up the scale until the sixth note (E) to find the relative minor key. To find the minor key that has two sharps, go to D major and locate the sixth note of that scale (B). It's pretty simple to work things out this way, and it's always good to know the relationships between related majors and minors.

7 INVERSIONS

This section of the book is designed to get more out of your playing, in particular to give it that extra bit of polish and solidity that will help you to sound more professional. As I said in earlier chapters, there's nothing wrong with having a simple, yet effective, technique. Good players rarely play everything at a million miles an hour – a big part of accomplished playing is knowing what to play and when to play it.

The first subject we're going to look at is chord inversions. To date, every chord we've played in the book has been in what's called *root position*. This is the basic starting point for a chord – if someone says, 'Play a C,' the chances are that they mean a root-position C. This introduces an area where keyboard players are at a significant advantage over other instrumentalists, such as guitarists. Because of the physical make-up of the guitar, certain notes are impossible (or extremely awkward) to play together. Furthermore, a guitar has only six strings, which further limits the amount of notes that can be played simultaneously. This means that a guitarist has great trouble playing all of the notes in many chords and therefore doesn't necessarily fully experience some inversions or root positions.

On a keyboard, there is substantially more flexibility, and therefore more to take on board. Despite this, however, understanding root positions and inversions is very simple, yet a lot of players haven't grasped exactly what they are and what a good knowledge of them can do for their playing.

Here's a root-position C chord:

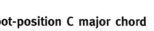

▲ Track 17

Root-position C major chord

This is pure textbook stuff. The right hand is playing a basic C major triad: C, E and G.

Now, if we take away the bottom C note and put it on top of the chord, we leave E at the bottom of the chord. Because we've rearranged the positions of these notes from the root chord, we have created an *inversion*.

C major first inversion (right hand only)

It's still a C chord, it still has the same notes, but it's called a *first inversion*, as we have the next-lowest note, E, at the bottom of the chord, while the C is now at the top of chord, one octave higher than in the root-position chord.

If we take the E away from the bottom of the chord and leave G as our lowest note, we have created another, higher inversion – a second inversion. Check out the following notation:

C major second inversion (right hand only)

Inversions can be created this way in any major or minor key. What does this mean for your playing? Well, very few pieces or parts use root-position chords from start to finish. (An exception can be found in early-'90s dance music.) Using different inversions gives much more contrast and dynamic interest to a piece and stops it from sounding stilted.

As an example, try playing the following chord sequence, which is all in root position:

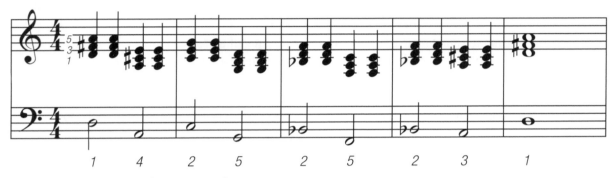

Backing-track chord sequence (root position)

Now play the same chords, but using the right-hand inversions below:

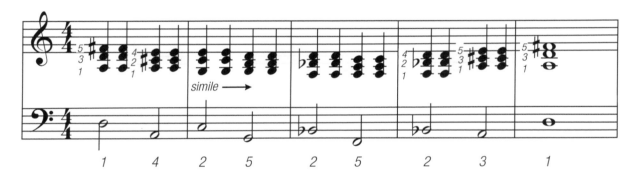

Backing-track chord sequence with inversions

There's quite a difference, don't you agree? Notice how not every chord is inverted; instead, there's a mixture of root position and inversions.

However, because we're playing with both hands, the above examples illustrate only partial inversions in the right hand. To perform a full textbook inversion, the bottom note of the chord should change as well, and with two hands this means the bass (left-hand) note if playing solo or the bass line in a group context. As you can see from the previous example, the left-hand (bass) part stays on the root notes while the right hand plays different inversions.

Therefore only partial inversions in the right hand, not full inversions, have actually been played, because the lowest note hasn't changed. When determining a chord's position – whether root position or inversion – it's always the bass (bottom) note that matters, whether playing with one hand, two hands or in a group with a separate bass line. This is where theory and practice often get muddled.

Most of the time, if you're reading a chord sheet it'll just say 'C, G,' and so on – it won't give details of inversions. In this instance, you can fairly safely assume that the bass notes will stay as root notes and the inversions that you play will be partial, confined to your right-hand parts, and it's up to you to decide whether or not to give them that extra colour and flavour.

If a chord chart asks your to play, for example, G major first inversion, it will almost certainly mean that the bass note is meant to come up to B. This doesn't mean that you necessarily have to play a first inversion with your right hand as well – judge what sounds better to you. Often, something like this would often be written as 'G/B' (often called *G over B*) instead, to avoid confusion.

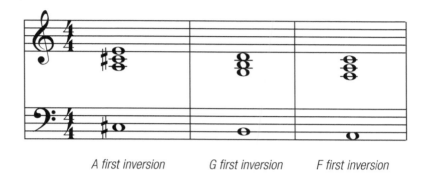

A first inversion   *G first inversion*   *F first inversion*

The right hand has stayed the same, but the bass part (left hand) has moved up to create first-inversion chords on the A, G and F. These are *full inversions*, distinctive in their sound. Often they seem as if they need to be resolved, as if waiting for another chord to be played.

So, how will you know when to use an inversion? Well, you'd usually have to deal with this if you were reading a chord chart, for instance (in which case you'd probably be confined to right-hand inversions, unless the music specifically directed otherwise), or writing your own music.

When playing along to a chord chart, listen to what the tune is doing. In this situation, you're accompanying the singer or instrumentalist, and your part should complement theirs, not override it. Often, chords and inversions that stay reasonably close to the tune, pitch-wise, work well.

For instance, look at the difference between the root-position and inversion examples above. The top notes of the root-position chords are all over the place. Imagine a tune being played or sung over that – it would sound a bit lumpy, to say the least. Now look at the example with inversions: the top notes of the chords stay within a much smaller area, and the part sounds smoother with it – much more suitable as a part.

I've written a simple tune with an accompanying chord chart. It has the same rhythmic feel as before. Try the chords in root position first, then experiment with a few inversions to hear and feel the differences in movement.

A simple tune with chord names annotated below the stave

As a starting point when making up inversions, try to make the top notes of the chords stay reasonably close to the tune. For effect, of course, you can do anything you like – and I firmly believe in experimenting!

That sums up chords and inversions quite well. There's no substitute for getting used to the sound of them and then trying out new ideas. For example, look at well-known tunes from pop music songbooks (which have chord charts underneath) and try out the root positions and inversions of all the chords. The more you do of things like this, the larger the steps you'll be taking towards finding a sound – and approach – of your own.

8 INTERVALS

In a music context, the word *interval* refers to the distance between two notes, usually within an octave. Knowing what basic intervals are is indispensable – we need to know what intervals are, and what they sound like, before getting into many more chords, as the names of the chords can refer to types of interval.

To help illustrate this, we'll look at our faithful C major scale. Counting the two Cs, one at the bottom and one at the top, we have eight notes. If I tell you that intervals can be called seconds, thirds, fourths, fifths, sixths, sevenths and octaves, you may well twig it straight away. For instance, if you want to know the interval (distance) between C and E, then count the notes: one, two, three – it's a third. Pretty simple. Likewise, the interval between E and A: one, two three, four – a fourth. It's important, though, to realise that an interval is the distance between *any* two notes, whether they're in the same key or not. I've used C major here only because it's a scale that's easily written down and viewed.

Track 18

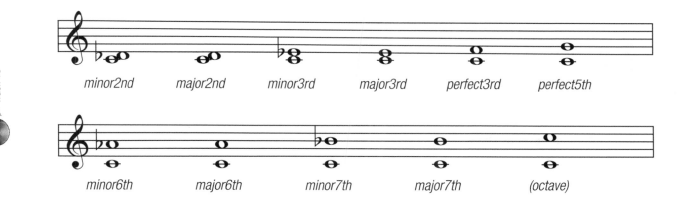

Basic intervals

While C to E is indeed a third, it needs something else to give it a full description. As you know, within a scale, each note has to have a different letter name, which is why you have a B♭ rather than an A♯ in F major, and so on.

So, while the interval between C and E is a third, surely C to E♭ must also be a third? It is. We therefore need to have a separate terminology where this occurs, and indeed each of these thirds is known by a different name. C to E is a *major third*, whereas C to E♭ is a *minor third*. Listen to them both and you'll hear the difference.

Seconds, thirds, sixths and sevenths all have major and minor intervals. Again, for reference purposes, have a look at the keyboard diagram on page 17, ascending from C. You can see that there's always one more semitone between notes of a major interval than between the notes of its minor version. Fourths and fifths are known as *perfect* intervals – because there's only one semitone between them, it's impossible to have major and minor versions.

More Tasty Chords

The major and minor chords that we've looked at so far are invaluable. You'll use them a lot of the time in the forms we've covered to date. But they're also building blocks to be used as a base, a point from which to explore and find new variations. The more types of chords you know, the more colour and dynamics you can put into your music. Also, you won't have to make excuses when you come to tricky bars in a chord chart...

Major Sevenths

The major seventh is sometimes thought of (and rarely used because of it) as something of a jazz chord. I love jazz, and I love major-seventh chords, but I use the major seventh equally when playing pop or rock music, too. The principle behind it is very simple: its name tells you what you need to know – a major chord with a seventh on top. Let's take D, for example – play a D major triad, as below, and the seventh note of the major scale, which is C♯. That chord is now D major seventh. Try this same procedure in other keys.

D major triad and major-seventh chord

Minor Sevenths

The minor seventh is a particularly useful chord and equally straightforward to work out. Let's find, for example, D minor seventh. Play a D minor triad, as below, and add the seventh note of the (pure) minor scale. Again, try this in other minor keys.

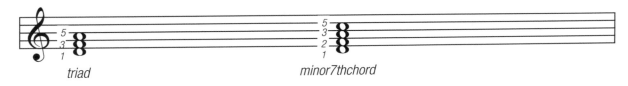

D minor triad and minor-seventh chord

Straight Seventh Chords

As we're on D for the other examples, let's stay on it to illustrate this variety of seventh chord, which would usually be called simply *D7*. It's essentially a major chord, using the same triad just as the major seventh above, but it has a flattened seventh as the top note.

Straight seventh chords and their variations are often used in blues.

D7 chord

They're also often used to resolve chord sequences back to certain keys. For example, if a piece was in G major and the last chord was G, a D7 would be a typical chord to play before the G in order to resolve the sequence, like so:

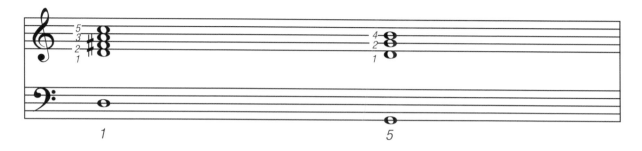

D7–G major progression

Notice that the interval between those two chords, D to G, is a perfect fifth. Remember, it is the movement of the bass notes that tells you this. This progression is often known as a '5–1' (or, more usually, 'V–I'). In this instance, '1' means the G, or key note, and '5' the D, as it's a perfect fifth above.

Elevenths

The name for this chord is derived from the interval between the bottom and top notes of the chord. Elevenths were at one time thought of as classic 'disco' chords, particularly in ascending sequences. Taking G11 as an example, we obviously have G as our bottom note. The rest of the chord is in the form of an F major triad, the last note of which is an 11th above the bass G.

You could obviously class this as F major over G – or F/G – and you'd be right. However, this could lead to inconsistencies, depending on which inversion of F you were playing, and it's this distinctive root-position F major chord with a top C – the 11th – that gives a G11, in this instance, the correct sound.

▲ Track 20

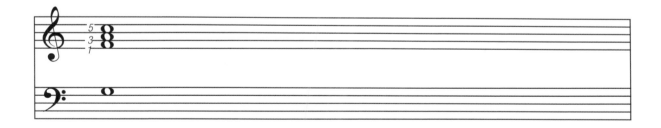

G11 chord

As a suggestion and a useful exercise for working out 11ths in other keys, find the 11th interval (an octave and a fourth, which is a perfect interval, so no major or minor versions) from the key note of the chord. This will be the top note of the major triad which forms the 11th chord.

Now, all of the chords I've shown you here are in their root, textbook forms. When reading lots of popular music or playing in a band, there will often be variations on how these appear. We've already seen with straight major and minor chords how inversions can make a lot of difference to the sound of the chord, particularly when playing along with a song, and of course you can invert all of the chords I've shown you here as well. Try changing their positions and exploring the changes in sound that result.

Also, when playing in a group of musicians, a guitarist's view of, say, Amaj7 would not be the version I showed you above. That's because he physically can't play the chord in that form, so he'll come up with a variation, which will essentially be that chord – maybe missing a note or two – and often inverting it slightly to make it possible to play. Be aware of this possibility when you come to find your own voicings.

9 RECOGNISING MUSIC BY EAR

'If you don't listen, you can't learn anything, in life or in music.' *Herbie Hancock*

Earlier on in the book, I said that being able to recognise chords and notes by ear is extremely important, and it certainly is. When we started to look at reading music from a stave, you were able to see what certain notes looked like on paper. That's actually quite helpful when ear training, because you start to get a mental image of which notes are higher or lower than others and what they sound like. A good start when recognising pitches of notes by ear is being able to find which area of the keyboard they belong to.

Identifying Intervals By Ear

To recognise notes by ear, it will help to familiarise ourselves with the sounds of the intervals we've encountered already.

Play a C on your keyboard and, without playing any other notes, try to hum a C major scale. Then take another note, at random, and hum a major scale from there. It's not too difficult, is it? That's because your memory has formed a good image of it. If you can't hum the scale at first, keep trying and you'll manage it soon enough without too much bother. Play along on the keyboard to help until you can rely on your brain.

The ability to hum a major scale is extremely useful when it comes to recognising intervals. Some intervals are more easily recognised than others, and you may have a good enough sense of pitch to identify some without going through this process. With the more difficult ones, it can take a little longer, but if you keep training your ear, it will come.

Each interval has its own sound, obviously, but looking at intervals within an octave, as we are at the moment, they fall into distinct groups:

- Major and minor intervals (seconds, thirds, sixths and sevenths);
- Perfect intervals (4ths, 5ths and octaves).

◀ Track 21

Major And Minor Intervals

Within the group listed above, it helps to divide them again into two types: seconds and sevenths, and thirds and sixths.

- Thirds and sixths form parts of root-position and inverted major or minor chords. As such, they sound pleasantly harmonic and are used a lot when harmonising, for instance, or when you're finding a part to play or sing beneath a tune.

- Seconds and sevenths have a more distinctive, dissonant sound. A minor second is a semitone, and therefore the smallest interval you can have in the 12-tone scale we use in Western music. A major second is one semitone bigger; again you can hear the clash as it sounds, but with a slightly more tonal sound to it.

▲ Track 22

Sevenths can often be found at the tops of root-position chords, as we've seen, making them into major sevenths, minor sevenths and straight sevenths. However, when a seventh interval is played on its own, either major or minor, it can sound much more dissonant than when it's part of a chord. For example, try playing a G major seventh and a G minor seventh, and then take away the third and fifth. Hear how different both the sevenths sound when played on their own.

Perfect Intervals

Perfect fourths and fifths have a clean, slightly 'spacey' sound. Taking the perfect fifth as an example, when this is played as part of a chord, such as a D major triad, this 'hollowness' is not as apparent. Remove the third to hear the fifth on its own, though, and you'll hear its characteristic sound.

Fifths are often used in left-hand parts because of their 'clean' sound. (We'll cover this more when we come to voicings of chords later on.)

Fourths have a similar, yet smaller, sound. To hear the interval within a chord, play a G major first inversion (D to G is a perfect fourth) and take away the B to hear the interval.

Try these exercises in different keys. Their varying colours can make the same intervals sound a little different until you're familiar with them.

Identifying Notes

Let's try a couple of experiments: on the CD, I'll play a note. Try to hum this note in your head. When you've done that, think what area of the keyboard it comes from. Is it high, low or in the middle? Again, when you think you've found the right area, try playing a few notes until you hit the same note as I've played on the CD. Repeat this a few times with the different notes I've given you.

Next, we're going to repeat this process, and afterwards I'll play another, higher note, which will be within the same major scale as the first one. Using the first, lower note as the tonic, hum up the scale until you reach the second note, then play the two notes together and see if you can hear and identify the interval. If not, don't worry – you can always refer to the keyboard diagram on page 17 to help you work it out.

Following this will be a series of notes which will be lower than the first, in a reverse of the above experiment.

To finish off, I'll play a series of intervals for you to identify. Don't panic if you can't recognise them by hearing their characteristics (and few people can until they've been doing it for a while) but work through the same technique – hum it, then find it and use a scale to work out which is the next note.

To develop your ear further, play intervals on your keyboard and make up your own chords. Get used to their sound. Look at pieces of music and see how the chords are constructed and used in conjunction with each other. This way, you'll probably find that you'll start to recognise parts of chords and intervals without having to work them out. Nothing is ever a waste of time, particularly when training yourself like this, so even if you feel you're getting nowhere – which can happen sometimes – just keep working at it and it will improve. People develop abilities at different rates, so don't be concerned if you need to take your time to work things out.

10 VOICINGS

'All music is important if it comes from the heart.' *Carlos Santana*

Track 24

In the previous chapter, we looked at how chords are basically comprised of a set of intervals, and how the sound of a chord changes when notes are removed, leaving certain intervals more exposed. With inversions, too, we've seen how the character of a chord can change when the notes are put in different positions. This reflects real-world playing well. All of the examples of chords and inversions we've encountered have been 'textbook' examples and, as I've said throughout the book, they are to be used as building blocks, a starting point for further exploration. In most circumstances, even when reading a piece, there will often be chord symbols written in above the notes. This is because a lot of the decisions regarding exactly which versions of a chord you should play are still down to you. To start to play effectively, we need to look a bit more carefully at how to voice chords – in other words, how to decide which notes and parts of chords to play, and which not to play…

Right- And Left-Hand Roles

Within the harmonic structure in a lot of popular music, both hands tend to have a fairly defined role. The right hand plays a tune and/or the principal chordal accompaniment; the left plays the bass plus other, more basic, chordal additions. There are exceptions, of course, but in the context of an accompaniment to a typical song, for instance, this is a common scenario. We therefore need to look at how to get each hand playing the kind of part that will sound right.

Let's take a typical triad – B minor. When played as shown in Example 1, it sounds light and clear but with a distinctly minor character. Move it down an octave (Example 2) and it has a deeper sound. Move it down another octave (Example 3), into the territory of left-hand playing, and it's starting to sound a little grotty. Down a further octave and it's decidedly unusable. This illustrates how the sounds of chords, and their voicings, change as we get lower down the keyboard.

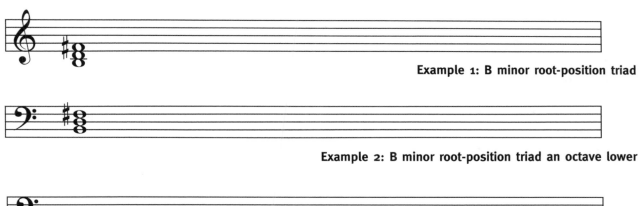

Example 1: B minor root-position triad

Example 2: B minor root-position triad an octave lower

Example 3: B minor root-position triad an octave lower

As a basic rule of thumb, you need to listen carefully to how chords (such as that B minor triad) sound once you've gone down past the C an octave below middle C. This is where an appreciation of how intervals sound and work with each other makes a lot of difference. The lower you go, the more you'll find yourself taking out thirds and sixths, leaving fifths and, particularly, octaves. While this on its own would mean that the chord had no reference to a major or minor key (with no third present), the right hand will usually be filling in that kind of harmony.

When both hands play the B minor chord together – the right hand playing a standard root-position triad around the middle-C area of the keyboard – see how the voicing of the left-hand chord changes the sound:

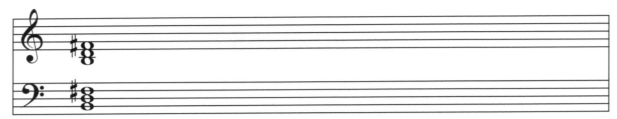

B minor triad (both hands)

B minor triad in right hand, fifth in left hand

You can hear distinctly the tighter, cleaner sound when playing the perfect-fifth interval in the left hand. Likewise, an octave in the left hand sounds similarly uncluttered and powerful:

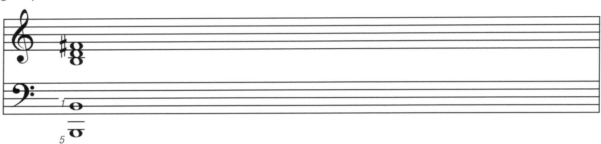

B minor triad in right hand, octave B in left hand

You can see how interpretation of chords is a two-handed business, and sometimes you need to take steps in order to avoid over-cluttering the sound. For instance, the left hand, usually playing the bass, will often contain part of a chord that doesn't need to be replicated with the right. The chord shown in Example 4 is a textbook root-position Gmaj7, and yet when playing with both hands you would naturally put a G in the left hand as the bottom note underpinning the chord. Therefore, you could leave out the G at the bottom of the chord in the right hand, leaving the upper three notes (Example 5). The difference in sound between the two is subtle, but it's a good example of how small changes in voicings can make a difference. When playing with other instrumentalists in a group situation, it's very useful to remember this and to be aware that taking notes out of a chord creates a marked change in the way it sounds.

Example 4: G major-seventh chord

Example 5: G major-seventh chord without tonic

11 PEDALLING

'The pedal is the soul of the piano.' *Anton Rubenstein*

Track 25

On an acoustic piano there are two pedals built into the lower casing. The left one is known as a *soft pedal*, which in the case of an acoustic upright piano moves the hammers closer to the strings and in a grand piano moves them across so that they strike only two strings instead of three. Many electronic pianos have a similar arrangement and approximation of effect, which is to give a softer, more delicate tone.

Sustain Pedal

Most electric pianos should have a sustain pedal attached, and if this is the case you might already be familiar with what yours does. That might suggest it's only for certain types of players, and I do see a lot of synth players who don't use one. Whether you've considered using one or not, I think it's one of the essential things to get to grips with and use properly, whatever style of music you play. Sloppy use of the sustain pedal sounds messy, but when used effectively it can be one of the main tools to benefit and polish your playing.

If your keyboard hasn't got a sustain pedal built in, the chances are it will have a socket at the back to accept one. It should be in the form of a normal quarter-inch jack socket, into which you plug the lead end of a separate pedal. These are readily available from most music shops and can be very cheap, although not always shaped like a piano's. However, as long as you can get a reliable feel on it and it doesn't slide around when depressed, that shouldn't matter very much.

So, when to use it? Well, let's try an experiment with the pedal attached and working. Press it down and hold while you play several notes at random. As its name implies, it will now sustain all the notes you play until it's released. Its most common use is to enable you to move from one chord to another with maximum smoothness. It can also be used for effect, as in our experiment, although this highlights one of the dangers of using the sustain pedal – it can easily be used in the wrong place and make a real mess of the sound.

As a rule of thumb, whenever it's needed, the pedal should be reapplied whenever the chord changes. Holding it down while you play two or more chords in different keys will sometimes cause dissonance, but if the same basic chord is held for a few bars holding it down can be effective. Care should be taken not to overuse it, though.

With chords, it's easier to grasp its usefulness, because when playing a chord with any number of fingers in either hand, when you have to move to another chord even a short distance away there will inevitably be a gap as you take your hands off the keyboard to play the next chord. With a sustain pedal, this isn't a problem. Depress the pedal while playing the first chord, holding the sound on. You're then free to take your hands off the keyboard and position them to play the next chord while the first chord is still sounding. Then release the pedal as you play the second chord. If done properly, the transition will be smooth and seamless.

To illustrate this, here's a quick example. Play one bar of an E major chord and one bar of A major, without pedal first:

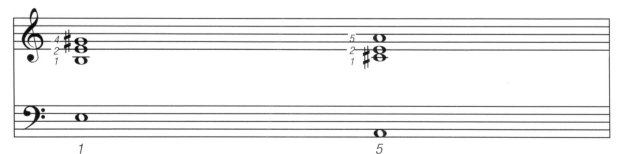

E major to A major progression

You can hear the gap during the change between the two chords, and it sounds a little awkward, so we'll depress the sustain pedal as we play the first chord. Now, moving our hands up to the A major, we can play the chord while releasing the pedal.

The important bit is the release of the pedal. If this is done too early, there'll still be a gap; too late and the two chords will blur together in an unpleasant way. The secret is to bring the pedal up at the same time as playing the next chord so that it becomes a simultaneous motion. At first it can seem strange doing this, as if you've left it too late, but with familiarity it will become second nature.

When the part in question has a bit more rhythmic activity to it than the previous example, the pedal can still be used. Imagine a typical pop-rock ballad, with the keyboard part playing a fours-type crotchet rhythm, such as that below:

repeat a few times

E major to A mjor progression with crotchet rhythm

Because the keyboard part is playing the same chord throughout each bar, the pedal can again be reapplied at the end of the first bar. As you're playing a chord on the last beat of the bar, however, be aware that there's far less time at the end of the bar to move your hand to the next chord. Repeat and go around the chord change a few times.

That's the basis of pedalling. With practice, it can be used during very subtle and rhythmically complex pieces of music. Once you've mastered the feel of it through playing simple parts, you'll find your technique with it growing as you develop your overall playing ability. Remember that pedalling is something that a listener should be largely unaware of, so use it accordingly.

You might find markings on pieces of music indicating where the use of the sustain pedal is required: underneath the bottom stave, a horizontal line will be drawn with two small vertical lines at each end to signify where it should be applied and released. Usually it will have a small 'ped' sign before it. However, unless you're playing pieces with dedicated piano parts, it's unlikely you will see this sign very often.

12 DYNAMICS

'It's not so much the sound of the instrument itself, it's like the
thing that you add onto it, the attitude.' *Keith Richards*

▲ Track 26

When music is created and performed, its purpose is to interest and inspire the listener, to create moods and colours, excitement and darkness. Music does this in many different ways, some of which we've looked at already, such as the different sounds of major and minor chords and the ways in which inversions can make chords of the same key change in character. Yet the main ingredient in making music really mean something is within the way it's played. Two different performers can make the same piece of music sound and feel completely different by use of dynamics.

The term *dynamics* means different things. To illustrate this at one end of the spectrum, think of a completely undynamic noise, such as a cheap electric alarm clock going off, making a monotonous single tone. Although the alarm has a pitch and is technically playing a note, it is not music, merely noise. And yet, when that same note is played on a keyboard, merely changing the way in which it's played can make it sound totally different.

This illustrates that there is rather more to music than just playing notes. It's the *feel*, the human element, that makes music tell a story and reach people. Otherwise, it would be nothing but a series of mechanical noises.

Out of all the indications of dynamic change on a piece of music, the most recognisable and easily understandable are known as *dynamic markings*. These are most commonly found in pieces of classical music, and are formally known by Italian names such as *forte* (marked f) and *piano* (marked p). Put simply, they mean *loud* and *soft*, respectively.

Think when you listen to music. The degrees of loudness and softness are varying all the time. They can be heard changing within a bar or a beat, or a section of music can change in dynamic over a long period, gathering energy or diminishing to nothing.

Within the type of pieces we've looked at so far, we can appreciate some of these changes and what they mean to the sound of a piece very easily. Let's look at something along the same line as the example we used for Chapter 7, 'Inversions'.

On the next page you'll find a straightforward 4/4 backing track (I've titled it 'Released'), a typical pop/rock ballad accompaniment. It's typified by the right-hand part playing a chord on every beat of the bar. Played without any dynamics at all, it sounds pretty awful and dull, as you can hear on the CD. And yet, with some thought and feel, it can sound completely different. To help apply this process, look at the basic information the piece gives you at the start. The tempo is the first indication – a slow piece will need a different approach from a fast one. The time signature is another – is it in simple or compound time?

Look at the key signature. Even if a piece is in a minor key, this doesn't necessarily mean it is slow and dull, any more than a major key has to reflect brightness. Instead, it's the movement of chords during the piece that gives it character and reference, as well as the types of chord used. So look at the chords that run through the piece and their duration. While this part is a fairly simple one that keeps a relatively steady movement of chords throughout, I'll illustrate how the feel of the piece changes very subtly, but importantly, within a few beats at a time.

Notice the lines that run above the music at the start of the piece for four bars at a time – these indicate the length of a particular phrase. Imagine talking for a couple of minutes at a time – you'd have to stop and take breath, wouldn't you? Phrasing markings can be interpreted in a similar manner – imagine them as guiding you to the length of a statement, after which you take an almost imperceptible breath. It's more felt than heard, but it's another important factor that helps music come alive.

Many songs and instrumental tracks like this run around a four-bar, 16-beat structure. It's one of the 'natural'-feeling durations within music that is used a lot. Dance tracks, on which parts are often brought in and out to give dynamics and inject excitement, commonly work around structures in groups of four – four bars doing one thing, something else brought in or taken out after another four, and so on. It's a formula that feels very comfortable within the human

'Released'

Tracks 27 & 28

Copyright © John Dutton 2002

body rhythm. This part conforms to this structure. Within the first four bars, the feel of the music can be heard to ebb and flow.

You can hear an emphasis on the first beat of bars 1 and 3. In a way, this is because it's answering the 'question' that is being asked during bar 2. The move to the minor chord in that bar changes the bright, sunny feel of bar 1, and it's almost as if it's asking the question, 'Where are we going?' The answer to this question is, back to the major chord at the start of bar 3 and the reaffirmation of the initial, brighter feeling. This happens again several times, and it's one of the many subtle variations within the piece that give it meaning.

The dynamic marking at the start of the piece is *mezzo forte*, marked *mf* (moderately loud).

And then, after eight bars, the piece moves onto another section, a bridge. *Bridge* is a term used somewhat loosely – a bridge is not of a pre-determined length and can occur anywhere in a piece. The term is commonly used to refer to a section of music that changes slightly from what has come before and either directs it to a chorus (in a typical song format) or reinstates the previous section (as in this case). Here, the bridge has a similar major-to-minor progression as the opening eight-bar section, yet the alteration of chords give it a feeling of change, another uncertainty. The dynamic markings change to reflect this, although not straight away. The term *dim* (*diminuendo*) tells you to quieten down gradually, so where this appears at the start of bar 14, bring the volume down until the next

dynamic marking, *mezzo piano* – marked *mp* (moderately quiet) – indicates that you've reached the required level.

The phrasing in the bridge reflects the change in the piece. Instead of occurring every four bars, the phrasing rises and falls over the first two bars (13 and 14), then each of the last two bars (15 and 16) is phrased separately. This gives a distinct feeling of a tiny pause for breath before bar 16, as if the music is gathering itself up to make a statement.

As the opening section is reinstated at bar 17, there's a natural feeling of release and energy. Because of this, the overall dynamic level of the piece changes in the last two bars of the bridge – *cresc* (*crescendo*) means getting gradually louder – and over those final two bars of the bridge the level grows from *mp* to *f*.

Over the last two bars of the piece, a feeling of *rallentando* (getting slower, usually abbreviated as 'rall') occurs. Think about it – most tracks that end with a dead stop, such as this one, don't just get to the end and stop with an abrupt halt. Instead the music wants to 'introduce' the end by easing back a bit. It makes the listener aware that the end of the piece has been reached.

So, although this is essentially a pretty straightforward progression of chords, it now sounds like a piece of music. It involves you, and the listener, to a degree that wouldn't have happened had you just played through the chords. Music must be more than a procession of notes and instructions – look into the music for the ebbs and flows, for the sometimes 'hidden' bits and colours that can be brought out.

13 PRACTISING

'I think we need to study things, and have musical experience before the word instinct *even applies. So, what I've said in the past is that I kind of view any musical endeavour like withdrawing from a bank account. The more that you invest over the years, the bigger the withdrawal you can make when it comes time to make that withdrawal.'* Lyle Mays

Practising – the very word brings a groan to some people. As a youngster, I would often loathe practising because I had to put in a certain amount of effort to keep up lessons. For a child, it can seem to be monotonous and boring. When you add to that the feeling that you're not getting anywhere sometimes, it's not surprising that some people give up or fail to put in enough time to improve their ability.

The term *practising* can have a negative feel to it, too – it suggests hours spent on your own, endlessly repeating exercises while everyone else is going out and having a good time. In any case, that kind of practice is not necessarily going to make for a good player.

So don't feel as if you're alone when you've just had enough or can't be bothered when it comes to practising. Everybody gets times like that. However, if you're like me, once I get started on something, I get into it and look forward to spending time on it everyday. And that's the crux of the matter – you might need to push yourself to get going, but once your interest is fired up, practising can become addictive.

As a professional, time spent with music is just what I do, and in fact I don't get nearly as much time to practise as I'd like. The reason I like to practise now is that I get a buzz out of learning and improving my abilities, because I know I'll never be able to reach a summit in playing – it's an infinite thing. The way that you'll get into practising is much the same. Once you feel improvement, and are able to put it into use, you start to feel the buzz and rise in self-esteem that goes with it. In life, we don't often get the chance to do things like that, sadly – at least, not with things that matter. With music, though, you're engaged in something artistic and creative, and that's a special feeling.

So when you need to motivate yourself to get up and spend some time with your instrument, think about these things. To be straight with you, doing something every day is the quickest way to improve – little and often, as I said in an earlier chapter. If you can get into this habit – and I mean half an hour a day upwards – you'll regard it as you would good posture and technique: it becomes a friend, a method of relaxation, that you can rely on. The only way in which you can't rely on it is if you're not bothered.

So, given this period of time of, say, half an hour, how is it best spent? Everybody's different, but breaking down your practice routine into areas can be a good idea.

Start off by getting comfortable, making sure that your posture is good and that you're relaxed and in control. A few exercises make for a good warm-up – you can refer to the ones in Chapter 2 and 3. Finish off with a few scales and arpeggios, maybe looking at a couple of keys you haven't done yet. That's a good half of the session gone.

When you're warmed up, look at a piece you want to play and work through it. Look at the chords, analyse them, see how the progressions move through different keys. Work through things slowly: if you start off playing something too quickly, the chances are it will always be scrappy. You need to train your muscles to perform new tasks when you play a new piece. You wouldn't take up running and immediately try to do a marathon, would you?

Don't forget to keep up your ear training. Listen to music that you know and try to hear what's going on. Find out what key it's in, see how the chords progress and are used. Through hearing music, you can learn so much, especially if you have in mind a lot of the things I've talked about in this book. Don't shut yourself off from styles of music you might not like straight away, either – a good playing style comes from appreciating a diverse range of music. To be good at anything – blues, pop, jazz, whatever – takes understanding.

Finally, don't look down your nose at anything. Instead, respect it and understand what you can. Very few things are a waste of time.

My parting words with practising are therefore that, in order to make progress on your instrument, a certain amount of discipline is required, but not at the expense of maintaining your enthusiasm, so make it as interesting as you can for yourself. And, as one of my teachers used to say, 'Slow practice makes for fast progress.'

14 GOING TO AUDITIONS

'I was so impressed, and maybe I wasn't sure if I wanted to play with them after all! The next day, they called and said, "You're in the band!" Funny business, auditions...' Patrick Moraz on his auditions for Yes

Auditions are, to many people, the musical equivalent of a driving test – a nerve-racking ordeal that goes past in a blur and you're not sure how the hell you got through it. For the inexperienced, only a true exhibitionist goes into such a situation supremely confident.

And that's why people like that rarely get on. What you must realise is that the people in an audition room (normally the other members of the band) are just human beings like you and are probably thanking their lucky stars they're not the ones having to audition. Someone who goes in completely full of himself stands a much greater chance of failing than a person who just tries to be himself and does what he can do to the best of his ability. Most good playing jobs in the industry, such as touring and session work, go to people who are easy to get on and work with. Of course, in that environment, having a certain degree of playing ability is a pre-requisite, but not every professional player is a flash harry; instead, they make sure that they're easy to work with and good at what they do.

And that's what you've got to do. Think back again to earlier chapters – when talking about technique, I made the point that there's nothing wrong with having a simple but effective playing style. Your ability is going to be taken into account when you think about what kind of group or situation you might be getting into. It might be a little early to go for that avant-garde modern-jazz fusion outfit, but you might feel as if you could do a good job in a group where you can put into practice what you know. So, in short, don't be over-ambitious too early. There's nothing wrong with stretching yourself a bit, but remember that you learn something from most playing situations, however simple the music may be that you end up playing.

Don't be afraid of being a bit nervous: a bit of fear, an edge, in these situations can be to your advantage. Use it, regard the whole thing as a bit of an adventure, and above all don't ever think that this is going to be the only chance for you. There's always something else to get involved in if you don't feel right about things. You're not the only one on trial; they are as well.

If, as is most likely, you have to ring someone up about a place in a group, be honest about what you feel you can do. It's good if you have common ground, such as similar likes and dislikes in music – pretty helpful if you want to enjoy playing with them. They'll probably want to know what kind of gear you've got – again, be honest and don't feel inadequate if you haven't got a bank of keyboards to bring along. You might have to learn a couple of songs in their set to audition with, and if so, make sure you know them. Fairly obvious, you might think, but incredibly some people do go along to auditions with absolutely no idea of what they were given to learn. Give yourself plenty of time to get there, and if you don't hear from them afterwards, so what? Chalk it up to experience and look for something else.

15 WHAT KIND OF GEAR DO I NEED?

This is one of the questions I get asked most often, and it's possibly the hardest to answer. It can be broken down a lot, though, by simply asking yourself, 'What kind of music do you want to play?' If you predominantly play piano music, occasionally trying out other musical directions, then a home keyboard or electric piano may contain enough features and sounds to satisfy your needs for a long time. On the other hand, a synthesiser keyboard will offer a much wider range of usable sounds and more flexibility, should you wish to expand your musical directions. Then, of course, you could maybe do with an electric piano and a synthesiser to cater for both eventualities. Welcome to the world of lusting after bits of musical equipment you can barely afford!

As well as a choice of piano sounds, an electric piano will usually have a limited selection of other instrument sounds on board. These are typically along the lines of strings, organ and, possibly, bass. I've often found that most of the effort has gone into making the pianos sound good and that the other sounds are something of an afterthought. While this isn't always the case, if having a large selection of high-quality sounds is your priority, I would consider a more general-purpose keyboard instead, or as well.

Aside from this choice, the only pre-requisites I'd place on equipment would be that it needs to have a MIDI interface, ideally with a General MIDI capability, and – in the case of a synthesiser keyboard or module – it should be multitimbral. These features are pretty essential these days, and even if you're not entirely sure what they mean, any reputable shop will steer you in the right direction. The chances are that, unless the keyboard/module in question is veering on the vintage side (over ten years old), it should be both multitimbral and MIDI-equipped.

How much do you have to spend? The fact is that these days most modern equipment is pretty amazing. The last decade or so has brought such an advance in technology that you don't need to spend very much money to get a keyboard or rack module that has excellent sound quality. The issue then becomes not so much what you have, but how can you get the most out of it?

16 THE ESSENTIALS

Essentials – what could they be? Well, just like in playing, there are different areas to know about within the technical side of electronic music, and sometimes it's assumed that you know what someone's talking about when in fact you haven't got the faintest idea! So, here's a brief nuts-and-bolts run-down of a few basic need-to-knows.

First, you need to know the leads that connect your keyboard. There are three primary types: mains, MIDI and audio.

Mains Leads

The unit will have either an integral cable or a socket at the back where you connect usually either a two-pin or three-pin lead. Three-pin leads are normally called *Europlugs* and are the same as you'd find on many kettles. Two-pin leads are the sort you'd connect up to your shaver or many portable hi-fi units.

MIDI Leads

We'll come to what MIDI is about very shortly. To be able to identify a MIDI cable, though, is an extremely basic thing – it's a lead with a five-pin DIN socket on each end.

Audio Leads

These come in a few shapes and sizes. If your keyboard has integral speakers and amplifier – such as most electric pianos and home keyboards – you won't need to connect any audio leads to make a sound. However, if you need to connect it to a source of amplification – to play with a band, for instance – you'll need to look at the outputs it has and connect it up the same way as you would a synth keyboard. A synthesiser doesn't normally have any built-in amplification at all (although you can use headphones).

Commonly, there are two types of output socket found on keyboards. Most usually – and almost certainly with a synthesiser keyboard – it will be a quarter-inch jack socket (it should be marked as 'Output' somewhere on the panel nearby). If you're having trouble finding the socket, it's about the same diameter as a drawing-pin head. A standard jack socket will be mono, characterised by one ring on the lead tip. Some electric pianos, however, have phono sockets, not jacks, for output. These are the same as you'll find on the back of a piece of hi-fi such as a CD player, and they're easy to recognise, as they're smaller than jack leads.

Connecting Up To Make A Sound

Now, what do connect your keyboard to? There are many options here, but we'll concentrate on two, firstly with an amplifier that's designed for the purpose. A typical keyboard amp would be a *combo*, meaning that the amplifier and speaker are all in one unit. Using one of these is simple: you just plug the jack lead from your keyboard into it and turn it up. If your keyboard has a phono output, you'll need to buy a small connector to plug into the end of your phono lead, which will then plug into the jack socket.

The other option is to go through a pair of hi-fi speakers or proper studio monitors. You can put your keyboard through your hi-fi amplifier – and thus your speakers – by connecting the output of your keyboard into a spare input on the back of the amplifier (maybe the 'Aux' socket) and turning it up. If your keyboard has a jack output, though, you'll conversely need to buy a small connector to plug onto the end of the jack lead to go into the amplifier, as most hi-fi sockets are phonos.

Most equipment these days can run in stereo or mono. Look at the output sockets on your keyboard – you may well have one with 'L' above it and another with 'R', meaning 'left' and 'right'. Both need to be connected if you want to hear what you're playing in stereo. The easiest way of doing this is through your hi-fi. You may have noticed that the input channel on the back of your hi-fi amp had two sockets, one white and one red. Connect the left output of your keyboard to the white socket of the amplifier and the right output to the red one.

If you're using a combo amp as described earlier, you'll need two of them to hear your keyboard in stereo. This is because the left and right outputs of your keyboard both need to be connected to a separate speaker (your hi-fi does this because the white, or left, socket is routed only to the left speaker and the red, or right, socket is routed only to the right speaker).

If you can run your gear in stereo, do so, because it almost invariably sounds better. In a rehearsal or gigging situation, where you may only have a single combo available, there are still ways around this – once we've looked at a few other issues first...

17 MIDI AND MULTITIMBRAL KEYBOARDS

'First of all, you have to be a musician in order to make music with a synthesiser.' *Robert Moog*

Earlier, I advised that any keyboard you buy should have a MIDI interface and be multitimbral. I'll now give you an introduction to what these things mean and what they can do for your playing and enjoyment of music. The important thing is not to be afraid! Take them one step at a time and you'll find that these are very exciting things to learn about and to put into practice.

What Is MIDI?

You can't hear it and you can't see it, yet it's probably the most important development in electronic music. These days, virtually every piece of musical hardware, such as a keyboard or effects unit, has a MIDI interface built in, and even if you play a basic home keyboard, those five-pin sockets are your gateway to a new world of musical experiences.

In spite of this, or sometimes because of it, many people are slightly fearful of exploring what MIDI can do. It's actually an incredibly simple facility, and I'm going to show you how useful it can be. First of all, I'll explain how MIDI (Musical Instrument Digital Interface) came into being and illustrate some of the things for which it can be used.

Rewind to the early 1960s. Electronic music was in its infancy and synthesisers were built around analogue, pre-transistorised technology. You may well have seen pictures of early synthesisers – huge pieces of metal hardware the sizes of a bookcases spewing forth myriad spaghetti-like leads. Tiny piano-type keyboards would be connected to these monstrosities in order to play them. By the end of the 1960s, an American inventor by the name of Robert Moog took advantage of the development of the transistor to design much smaller synthesisers (such as the classic Minimoog) which were also considerably cheaper.

Minimoogs and similar units from rival companies became extremely popular and started to feature prominently in pop and rock music. There were drawbacks to these early keyboard synths, however, the main one being that, due largely to their analogue control interfaces, they were *monophonic* (ie they could play only one note at a time).

Fast-forward to the end of the 1970s and things were looking a bit different. Some keyboards could now play several notes at one time (ie they were *polyphonic*) and digital technology was becoming cheaper. The yards of spaghetti described earlier could now be replaced by digital circuits and control panels. Before the end of the decade, the first entirely digital synthesisers had appeared.

With these advances, there was an opportunity to design an interface that would enable digital equipment to communicate with other, similar units and be used and controlled from a single source – a single keyboard, for instance. Rather fortunately, the various manufacturers all decided on a common system to allow this to happen and MIDI was born. Consequently, from the mid-1980s onwards, virtually every keyboard, from humble electric piano to top-of-the-range synthesiser, has been built with a MIDI interface.

The MIDI Effect

Without explaining any more, let's pitch straight into a real-life scenario. You have two keyboards: Keyboard A and Keyboard B. Each has a MIDI interface.

You go to your local music shop and buy a standard five-pin MIDI cable. You plug one end into the socket marked 'MIDI Out' on Keyboard A. You plug the other end into the socket marked 'MIDI In' on Keyboard B. Providing both keyboards are set to the same MIDI channel, and both are connected to an amplifier and speakers, when you play any note on Keyboard A, the same note on Keyboard B will sound as well. When that note is played on Keyboard A, you're generating a MIDI signal, which is transmitted through the MIDI cable to trigger Keyboard B. (Of course, this is not limited to one note – you can play any number of notes or chords in this manner and MIDI will transmit them all.)

Notice that Keyboard A is acting as the *controller*, and that the cable is plugged into the MIDI Out. That's because you're playing a note, and therefore sending information out of Keyboard A, and that's why the cable is plugged into the MIDI In of Keyboard B, the *slave*, as it is receiving information. This basically explains two of the three MIDI sockets you commonly find on the backs of keyboards. We'll come to what the other socket, 'Thru', does in a moment.

It is important that you understand what MIDI is doing here. It does not transmit *sound*; it transmits *information*. In essence, when you play that note on Keyboard A, it is sending a message through the cable to Keyboard B, telling it to play that same note. If you turned down the volume on Keyboard B and triggered again it from Keyboard A, it would still receive the MIDI message but would not make a sound. You would have to turn up Keyboard B again to hear it, just the same as if you were playing it directly. All the MIDI signal is doing is remotely controlling Keyboard B.

Because of this ability to control other instruments and devices from a single keyboard, it is common these days to buy *modules* – versions of keyboards that come in a standard rack-mounted form – with no integral keyboards. All the sounds and features of the module are exactly the same as the equivalent keyboard, and all its functions – note information to make it sound, as well as other MIDI data – can be controlled from the master keyboard. This saves space in a studio or live environment. Modules are so popular now that several don't have keyboard equivalents.

The above is a very simple example of what MIDI can do. Its usefulness spreads much wider than merely triggering notes on another keyboard. After all, a MIDI message such as that note information is basically data – binary code – comprised of 0s and 1s. Most keyboards can transmit other messages as well as note information – for instance, if you changed a voice on the controller keyboard, it would send a message through the MIDI cable to the slave keyboard and the slave would also change voice accordingly (if set up to do so). The same goes for movements of the pitch-bend and modulation wheels and the sustain pedal. In fact, just about anything you operate on a modern keyboard can be sent out as some kind of MIDI message.

Using MIDI To Record Music

However, you're not limited just to sending information to another keyboard. This is where MIDI gets really interesting. As I said at the start of the chapter, virtually all modern musical pieces of electronic equipment have MIDI interfaces. These days, most computers also have facilities to receive

MIDI signals, and by using sequencer programs they can be used to record and play back MIDI note information.

Some keyboards have sequencers built in, although these are often of a fairly limited capability. More usually, a sequencer will either be in hardware form (a small metal box) or software form (such as the computer-based program mentioned above). While hardware sequencers were popular in the early days of MIDI, most sequencing is now done on computers, for a number of reasons.

As an example, though, I'll use a hardware version to describe the basic operation of a sequencer. A hardware sequencer would typically be about the size of a large A4 book, have a row of buttons with transport controls (Play, Record, Fast Forward and Rewind) and a MIDI interface, with MIDI In and MIDI Out. That's all we're concerned with for now.

Referring to the earlier example with Keyboards A and B, we're going to leave the MIDI lead in Keyboard A's MIDI Out socket but remove it from Keyboard B's MIDI In. We're going to put it into the MIDI In of the sequencer instead. Therefore, the keyboard is still our controller and we're going to send out note information through the MIDI Out socket. The sequencer is going to receive this information through its MIDI In.

While normally you would set a tempo on the sequencer, that isn't actually necessary for the purposes of this example, so all that's needed to record music is now to check that both the keyboard and the sequencer are on the same MIDI channel and to press Record on the sequencer. Whatever you now play on the keyboard will be transmitted through the MIDI cable to the sequencer and stored as note information (data) within the sequencer. (Remember, MIDI deals with information only.)

When you press Stop on the sequencer, you'll want to hear your masterpiece back. However, the MIDI connection is going out from the keyboard into the sequencer. To hear back what you've recorded, you'll need to connect another MIDI cable (or swap around the original if you were too broke to buy two), this time going out of the sequencer and into the keyboard. Then, provided that they're both on the same channel, when you press Play on the sequencer, it will transmit the note information you recorded onto it back to the keyboard, and the keyboard will play.

18 MIDI CHANNELS AND SEQUENCING

When explaining how basic MIDI situations worked in the previous chapter, I made reference to MIDI channels. MIDI has 16 separate channels, all of which can transmit and receive data simultaneously, independently of each other. Within the scope of what I've already illustrated, there seems little point in having 16 channels – surely just one would do?

The simple fact is that we've only scratched the surface of what MIDI can do. When you start to explore multitimbrality, you're opening up another new area of possibilities and you'll soon understand the need for more than one MIDI channel. In fact, it will become clear that 16 are often not nearly enough...

Multitimbral literally means 'many sounds' and describes the ability of a keyboard, or module, to play back several sounds at the same time. A modern synthesiser, for example, has a substantial array of sounds, from pianos through to basses, brass instruments and drum kits. With a multitimbral keyboard, you can assign up to 16 different sounds and record and play them back on any of the 16 MIDI channels. In order to do this, you need to use a sequencer, and these days the easiest and best way of doing it is to hook up to your PC or Macintosh.

You see, the simple hardware sequencer I looked at in the previous chapter isn't the most user-friendly thing around. Often the only display you have on these models is a tiny screen, and in terms of computing power they're way behind what modern computers can do. So, if you haven't bitten the bullet yet and tried making music with your PC, then now is a good time to start. The chances are that it will involve only a very minimal amount of expense, and it will take less time to get comfortable with it than you thought.

Hooking Up To A PC

One of the problems of a book like this is that there is often a wide disparity between equipment at people's disposal. One of the key issues where computers are concerned can be whether you use a PC or Mac. Lots of people within the industry use Macs, and many people have them at home,

too. However, I suspect that most of you will be using a normal home PC, at least at the moment, and while advice is relevant to both PCs and Macs, there are some operating differences which may crop up when using a Mac.

The power of a modern PC is more than enough to supply all your likely needs for recording at this stage. Anything above 400MHz with a hard drive of 10Gb should be sufficient – ample to give you space to store recordings. Obviously, the damned things get quicker all the time, so even a fairly recent model can be OK.

The very basic operation of a music sequencer program is similar to standard word-processing programs you may have used on a computer before. Some of the menus at the top will be the same – File, Edit and Help(!) – so you can get a feeling for your surroundings quite easily. But before you're able to start recording and playing back files, we need to look at what kind of hardware you have on your computer.

The most essential thing you need right now is a means of getting a MIDI signal in and out of the computer. Unlike a standalone sequencer computers don't have built-in MIDI sockets, so your computer will need to have a soundcard, a device that enables you to plug your keyboard into the computer. A lot of computers have built-in, integral soundcards which will do the job for now. You will need to buy a cheap 'Y' cable, one end of which will plug into the soundcard's joystick port. On the other end of the cable will be a pair of MIDI leads which you connect to your keyboard. Put the cable marked Out into your MIDI In and the cable marked In into your MIDI Out.

If your soundcard is properly installed, you should have enough hardware connected to be able to start basic MIDI recording. Other methods are available, such as using a USB device, but we'll come to these later.

Programs

Again, one of the difficulties with this subject is that things change so quickly and new programs come out all the time. I'm going to give you enough information on the type of program you need to use – a multitrack sequencer – to get you started and get you to appreciate the multitimbral capability of your keyboard, if so equipped. Even if your keyboard is not multitimbral, you can still get a lot of use out of the sequencer, so read on.

When you've loaded the sequencer program and it's running on your desktop, if you play a note on your keyboard it should register as being received by the sequencer. This will probably be in the form of a little bar lighting up as you depress and release the note, just to reassure you that it's connected and working. Most programs have a series of vertical tracks running from top to bottom of the screen, and in the default setting that these go to when first loaded, they'll probably select track 1, which will also usually be set to MIDI channel 1. Your keyboard, unless you've altered it, should also be set by default to MIDI channel 1. Therefore, with everything on the same MIDI channel and a MIDI signal being received, you can start recording.

Put the program into Record mode and play a few notes. When you've finished, stop the program. (Most scroll horizontally when playing back or recording, so something should have appeared on-screen when you were recording.) Now press Play. Provided your keyboard is connected to an amplifier, you should hear what you recorded.

Again, you must understand what's going on here. Your computer is playing back only note information – it hasn't recorded any audio. The audio you're hearing is coming out of the keyboard's output socket, just as if you were playing it. The computer is playing back the note information you recorded into it, through your keyboard. If you used a sustain pedal, your computer will also have recorded the information generated when you depressed and released it – this is a type of *controller information*. Each control change you make on the keyboard, be it via sustain pedal, pitch-bend or modulation wheel, patch change – in fact, just about anything – has a dedicated controller-information number and can be recorded onto the sequencer, either as you play notes or afterwards, when your computer's playing back.

So now you have a track to play back on the sequencer. To add to it, check that the sequencer isn't set to replace the track and you can record another part on a different track, as long as the MIDI channel is adjusted to 1 – you'll

then hear both. However, this is a little restricting, as you'll have selected only one sound. To go further, you need to get into multitimbral operation.

Multitimbral Operation

First of all, this requires you to take a closer look at your keyboard. As I've explained, some older keyboards may not have this facility, nor will a lot of electric pianos or home keyboards. Multitimbral synthesisers started to appear in the late 1980s, but some equipment produced much later may still have only a limited facility.

At its best, multitimbral capability enables you to assign a different voice to each of the 16 MIDI channels over which your keyboard can transmit and receive. Some earlier or lesser machines may have enough power to assign up to only six or eight voices. That doesn't necessarily matter too much.

A multitimbral keyboard usually has two modes it can be set in for normal playing. One is often called *Patch mode*, whereby you select the various sounds the instrument has, one at a time. The other is called *Performance mode*, and in this mode you can start to assign several different sounds at once. This is a slightly different procedure, depending on which manufacturer's keyboard you're using, but the principle is the same. You will be able to select up to 16 *parts* (each with a different sound, if you wish) within a single performance and give each of them whichever MIDI channel you desire. (It's possible to give them all the same channel, if you want to.)

Now, for the purposes of this exercise, assign part 1 to a piano sound and set that part to MIDI channel 1. When you go back to your sequencer, make sure that the track selected is set to MIDI channel 1, and you can play and record exactly as you did before.

Set part 2 on your keyboard to a bass sound, for example, and to MIDI channel 2. Select or create a new track on the sequencer set to MIDI channel 2, and when you record the bass part you'll hear the piano part being played back on channel 1 at the same time. The parts are completely separate from each other, just as they would be on a multitrack tape recorder. You can then do this with up to 16 sounds, enabling you to create or play back a very full-sounding track.

19 GENERAL MIDI

Fairly early on in the days of MIDI, it became clear that, even though the basic principle of controlling other manufacturers' instruments via a MIDI interface worked, several details needed to be ironed out. One of the most typical was the difference in patch-numbering systems between different manufacturers. As I've explained, when selecting a patch on the controlling instrument, the slave also changes, if set to do so. All very well, but the only problem was that patch numbers between different makes of instrument weren't universal. Patch 10 on a Roland keyboard wasn't the same sound as patch 10 on a Yamaha, for example.

This made the construction of MIDI files particularly awkward. In theory, if every manufacturer used the same patch numbers for the same sounds, a track could be made up on a sequencer, with appropriate program and patch changes, and it could be played back on any multitimbral, MIDI-equipped keyboard. As we can see above, this was beset by inconsistencies between different makes of keyboard. A lot more standardisation was necessary to make this a reality, and so the idea for General MIDI was born.

With manufacturers agreeing to standardise patch numbers to certain sounds and create a recognised sound set, where a standard was set for 128 patches to appear in a certain order, under the new General MIDI protocol it was now possible to create compositions that could be saved on a MIDI sequencer as GM files and played back on any GM-equipped keyboard, irrespective of the manufacturer. The one requirement was that the keyboard used to play back the GM file was fully multitimbral; in other words, it could receive and play back 16 MIDI channels at once, each with a different GM patch. So, if playing back MIDI files is a priority for you, ensure that the instrument you buy is fully multitimbral.

Listening to other people's MIDI files can be quite good fun, and useful, too. When you import a MIDI file into a sequencer program, it's handy to see how they've programmed the song. Of course, the quality of files varies enormously – you can, at one extreme, buy professionally produced MIDI files that are made to a very high standard, while at the other you can download an endless number from the internet. If you are doing this – and most musicians have done at some point – bear in mind the usual provisos about viruses and hidden content, particularly as the file will come as an attachment.

20 POLYPHONY AND VOICE RESERVES

The term *polyphonic* describes the ability of an instrument to play several notes at once. In a keyboard context, it seems difficult to understand now how anything else could be of much use...

Polyphony is not a limitless feature, however. All keyboards and MIDI modules have a limit on the number of notes they can play at one time. A modern instrument can manage up to 128, whereas merely a few years ago some would struggle to manage 32. When you're using a keyboard in a multitimbral capacity, it's surprising how quickly you can use up those notes. You can usually hear when polyphony is starting to be stretched – transitions between chords and notes 'snatch' and the sound loses a lot of its normal effortless quality. However, there are ways to maximise your machine's capabilities, namely by using the 'voice reserve' function.

Voice reserve enables you to determine how many notes are 'assigned' to each part. In a machine with 64-note polyphony, this allows four per part, if using all 16 parts at once – when you're listening to a MIDI file, for instance. If you think about how much data a piano part can use up on its own, when playing chords and using the sustain pedal, it would clearly need a larger allowance than four notes. On the other hand, a bass part, playing a single note most of the time, could easily make do with less than four, as could any other part that uses only one or two notes at a time.

21 CONNECTING INSTRUMENTS VIA MIDI

The third MIDI socket on your keyboard can be used in a number of different ways. Taking our initial, basic example from Chapter 17, where we controlled one keyboard from another using a single MIDI cable, a further keyboard can be controlled by linking it through the slave unit's MIDI Thru socket. This third keyboard can then be controlled in the same way as the original slave. This daisy-chain method can be further extended to include other MIDI-equipped devices.

Basically, the Thru port passes on all the information that comes into the MIDI In socket and transmits it to the next device. If you're considering using two or three MIDI-equipped devices on a regular basis, you may find it worthwhile considering a multiple-port MIDI interface, which will make your life a lot easier. Honestly!

Multiple-Port MIDI Interfaces

If you have only one keyboard, then you're unlikely to need more than the 16 MIDI channels we've already encountered. However, if you have more than one instrument, or even just another MIDI-equipped device, such as a drum machine, then you may soon realise the limitation of having just 16 channels. Let's presume that you have a couple of keyboards and have used one of them to recorded a track that uses all 16 MIDI channels. This means that, if you wanted to record another few MIDI tracks using the other keyboard, there would be no spare channels.

Fortunately, there is a way around this. The method of connecting your keyboard that I described earlier – using the joystick port – usually works OK but is limited in that it restricts you to 16 MIDI channels. These days, a separate USB MIDI interface is worth looking at because it's cheap, easily installed and can offer a number of separate MIDI ports. A USB MIDI interface is a small box that simply plugs in to one of the USB ports on a computer at one end and, at the other, has a number of MIDI sockets to which you can connect your equipment. Most USB interfaces of this type have more than one 'port', meaning that you have multiple (usually at least four) MIDI Ins and Outs, meaning up to 64 MIDI channels. You can select which port to use on the sequencer program.

The beauty of this arrangement is that you can have one keyboard set up permanently, and once it's connected you can use it to control other MIDI gear without having to plug and unplug MIDI cables. With a USB device, the proviso is that your computer has to be switched on in order to power it, but the chances are that it would be anyway if a sequencer program was being used (and some run on batteries as well).

22 SETTING UP YOUR GEAR

At some stage, many of you will want to put into practice what you know and start rehearsing with a group and performing on-stage. This brings its own set of issues, both practical and technical.

Setting Up Your Keyboard

For rehearsal purposes, in order to hear yourself it will be necessary to have something along the lines of the combo amp discussed earlier. These models have the advantage of being very self-contained, so all you need to do is plug it in, connect a jack lead from your keyboard and turn it up to get a sound. They should also be loud enough (I'd get something around 100 watts) to hear what you're doing in a rehearsal room while a guitarist is wailing away and the drummer is knocking pieces out of his kit.

However, when you get to a gig situation, things may be quite different. Obviously, a gig situation can be anything from someone's front room to a small club, a theatre or a larger venue. In anything apart from the smallest gigs, your combo won't have enough power or projection for you to be heard. In these circumstances, a PA (Public Address) system will usually be provided, so that you and the other members of your ensemble can all be heard. PA systems vary enormously in size and capability, but they all follow the same principle – a set of speakers each side of the stage, pointing out towards the audience, through which the band is heard. Very small PA systems are sometimes suitable only for vocals, but in most circumstances they will be big enough to put your keyboards through.

So, how does this happen? Well, there are several ways to cook this egg. Your combo will almost certainly have a Line Out socket somewhere on it called a DI (Direct Inject), and a lead can be taken from that and given to the PA engineer. This sends a feed from your combo to the PA. However, this way you're not making the most of the sound of your keyboard – it's in mono and you're restricted in how much you can turn yourself up on-stage, because whenever you turn up you will correspondingly send more signal out

through the DI socket to the PA, possibly causing distortion problems and earning you an earful after the gig.

In my opinion, there's a better way, allowing you to retain as much control over your sound as you need and still ensure that the signal getting to the PA is of as high a quality as possible. However, some very modest expenditure is necessary.

I'd suggest you purchase a small mixing desk – one with either six or eight input channels would be perfectly adequate – which has at least one auxiliary send (I'll come to that in a moment). Most mixing-desk manufacturers make such models, and they are usually of good quality and useful in several other situations as well as live performance.

Such a desk will be very easy to use. Whether it has six, eight or more input channels, typically it will have a fader for each input channel and a fader on the right-hand end to control the master volume. Some very small 'notepad'-type desks don't have faders, only knobs, which is OK, but using these is sometimes less immediate when things are dark on-stage and you need to adjust something in a hurry.

Input channels are easy to understand – each one can have a single mono input plugged into it, such as a lead-out from your keyboard or a microphone. An input channel will usually have the following controls (from the top of the channel downwards):

- **Gain** – If this is turned to zero, you won't hear a sound. Turn it up slowly to increase the level of your instrument coming into that channel;

- **Equalisation (EQ)** – Typically, this comes in the form of three knobs marked High, Mid and Low. Use these in much the same way as those on a home hi-fi to change the tone of the sound (if necessary);

- **Auxiliary Send (Aux)** – The desk may have one or two of these knobs. As the name suggests, it sends out the signal from that channel to allow connections to be made to another piece of equipment (I'll come to this in a moment);

- **Pan** – Used to control which side of the stereo speakers you want that sound to come from;

- **Fader** – Brings up the volume level of a channel;

- **Master Fader** – Controls the overall volume of the desk.

One of the advantages you may notice straight away with a desk is the ability to run in stereo. Most keyboards sound infinitely better in stereo – if in doubt just listen to it on headphones. If your keyboard has a straightforward left and right output you can put the left one into desk channel 1, for instance, and the right one into desk channel 2. Provided they are both turned up to the same level, the only thing you'll need to do to make sure these run in stereo is to turn the pan knob on channel 1 all the way to the left and the same knob on channel 2 all the way to the right. That way you have only the left output of the keyboard sound coming through the left side of the desk and the right output coming through the right side of the desk. To connect your desk to the PA plug a pair of leads into the master output sockets on the back of your mixing desk and give them to the PA engineer. Make sure he knows you're running in stereo.

Plugging in a pair of headphones into the desk can be very useful as a way of hearing what's going on, particularly when needing to tell if you're running in stereo or mono.

Hearing Yourself On-Stage

The next question is, how do you hear yourself? You've plugged your keyboard into your mixing desk, given the outputs of your desk to the PA engineer and your expensive combo amp is lying in the corner feeling sorry for itself. Well, it's still going to be used, but it will have to be connected in a different way to the way it was before. This is where you'll find that the auxiliary-send feature is indispensable.

Usually called a 'send' or 'aux', the auxiliary send enables you to feed a separate signal from your desk to the combo. On the rear panel of the desk, there will be a socket marked 'Aux' or 'Aux Send'. If the desk has more than one auxiliary send, for these purposes just use aux 1. The Aux socket on the desk is usually a normal jack type – connect a jack lead from this Aux socket to your combo. Make sure the combo is turned up.

Presume that one of the outputs from your keyboard is going into channel 1 and that you can hear yourself through the main outputs of the desk (using headphones would do), turn up the Auxiliary Send knob on channel 1 and you should hear it coming out of your combo. You can adjust the level of send on the desk or the volume on your combo to make it louder or quieter.

Any changes you make to your Auxiliary Send knob won't alter the levels coming out of your desk's master output. The auxiliary is a completely separate feed. Therefore, in this way you can make the most of your stereo sound by giving your mixing desk master output to the PA and still have complete control over your own volume on stage.

This type of little desk can be extremely useful. At home, you can connect up the master outputs to your hi-fi and run several instruments through it in stereo. Spare input channels can be used to plug in other instruments or microphones as well. It's possible to pick up a new desk that will do the job for anything between £80 and £200. Second hand, they can go for peanuts.

23 GENERAL ADVICE FOR GIGGING

Doing a gig can be a great buzz, but for many people it can also be very stressful, meaning that they rarely perform to their maximum. This can be due to several reasons, including everybody playing too loudly. This is easily done. In fact, every musician's done it on at least one gig (and often in rehearsal rooms, too). When you're performing live, it's very easy to get carried away. You're (hopefully) performing in front of a crowd often containing your friends and family. While one of the reasons for getting louder can be that it sounds more exciting, another factor can be that it masks a performer's anxieties – there can be a feeling of added security when you make more volume – yet this lures you into a false sense of safety and makes most problems worse. If you find yourselves needing to do this, it's better to address the cause of the problems and avoid getting into bad habits with tension, such as those discussed in earlier chapters.

Before you perform on-stage with a band, you'll have had a soundcheck before the gig to check that everyone's connections to the PA are working correctly and for the engineer to mix all the different instruments through the PA system. On-stage, there will be a number of triangular speakers called *wedges* projecting up from the floor, and these project the sound back to vocalists or other members of the band. Try to get a level that everybody in the soundcheck is comfortable with and keep it there for the gig.

The sound of a room can change between the emptiness of a soundcheck and a packed audience when you come to play. This often causes members of the band to panic and think that they must turn up in order to be heard. This is the worst thing they can do. Remember, the PA (the sound out front) is making the real meat of the noise – turning up too much on-stage does nothing except unbalance the sound.

You can't get an accurate idea on-stage of how the gig sounds out front. The main speakers are pointing away from you, after all. I've done gigs during which I thought,

on-stage, that the sound must be terrible out front only to have several people come up and say it was the best they'd heard the band play! Because the sound on-stage is set up primarily to allow the band to hear themselves, having a perfect mix is not always possible. Don't confuse that with a poor sound out front. Instead, relax and allow yourself to feel confident in not needing to be at excessively loud (and ear-damaging) levels.

From time to time, you may have to perform tracks that you have a problem with playing. For instance, one might have an awkward section that you can't master or a solo you can't manage yet. This is where, if it's too far beyond your capabilities, you have to be honest and admit that you'd rather not do it. If you end up having to do it anyway, you need to find a way of getting through it. How?

If it's an awkward passage of chords, think about the number of notes you are playing. As we've seen, it's possible to leave out notes that are superfluous to the sound, so listen and think about which are the really crucial notes and see if you can rework the harmony around those. If the difficult part is confined to one hand, notice what the other hand is doing – you might manage it if you use both.

When you've found an acceptable compromise, practise it slowly for as much time as you can. Remember the phrase 'get your form right'. The track may still be extremely difficult to play, but you'll be giving yourself the best chance if you practise it slowly until you need to play it up to speed. The results may surprise you...

If you're having trouble with a solo, again try to break it down. You can probably manage some of it without a problem, so concentrate on the difficult section. Most solos are worked around some sort of scale, so look at the fall of the notes and see if you can identify a key, arpeggio or scale that you know already. Doing this may make you realise that it's not quite as bad as you think – if you can rattle off the scale or arpeggio without a problem, then surely it can't be that bad? Again, practise it slowly. This really is the best way around it.

GLOSSARY

Below is a selection of terminology, both musical and technical, that I've used throughout the book. It is by no means a comprehensive dictionary, but it'll hopefully help some things to slot into place.

Accidental – Rudimentary term describing a sharp or flat.

Arpeggios – The notes of a chord played separately in succession.

Ascending – Describes the movement of notes going up in pitch.

Auxiliary Send – A feature on a mixing desk's input channel that enables a signal to be sent to a separate, auxiliary output.

Bar Line – The point marking the division of beats within a given time signature.

Beat – The pulse, or measure, that runs through a bar.

BPM – Abbreviation of *beats per minute*, used to describe the speed, or tempo, of music.

Bridge – An intermediate or transitional section of a piece of music.

Chord – A selection of at least three notes played simultaneously.

Combo – An amplifier and speaker contained in a single, combined unit.

Compound Time – Time signature in which each beat is divisible by three.

(MIDI) Controller – Instrument or other MIDI-equipped device that sends out MIDI information.

Crescendo – Indicates that music should get gradually louder.

Descending – Describes the movement of notes going down in pitch.

Diminuendo – Indicates that music should get gradually quieter.

DIN – Multipin connection on the end of a lead used to transmit and receive MIDI signals.

Dissonance – Describes the sound of atonal (clashing) harmonies.

Double Bar – Two bar lines written together to indicate the end of a piece of music.

Dynamics – The graduation of musical loudness and softness.

Eighth Note (Quaver) – A note that has the time value of half that of a quarter note (crotchet). In a 4/4 time signature, there are eight quavers to a bar.

EQ – Abbreviation of *equalisation*, the increasing or decreasing in volume of specific frequencies or bands (typically high, mid and low).

Europlug – A power lead with a plug on one end and a three-pin female socket on the other (as on many kettles).

Fader – Vertically-moving control on a mixing desk that alters the signal volume on a particular channel and, in the case of a master fader, the overall desk volume

Female – Describes a connection on a lead or socket of whatever type – audio, mains, MIDI, etc – that has one or more recesses to accept a male (protruding) pin or pins.

First Inversion – The first specific rearrangement of the notes in a chord when ascending from root position.

Flat – A sign (♭) which, when placed before a note, lowers it by a semitone. When a voice or instrument is sounding below correct pitch, this is also known as 'being flat'.

Forte – Italian musical term for 'loudly'.

Full Note (Semibreve) – A note with the time value of four quarter notes (crotchets).

Gain – Knob on a mixing desk (usually at the top of an input channel) that controls the amount of level accepted into that channel.

General MIDI – A set of standard requirements for MIDI devices to ensure consistent playback of certain data, such as GM format MIDI files.

Half Note (Minim) – A note twice the length of a quarter note. In a bar of 4/4, a half note lasts for two beats.

Input Channel – Section of a mixing desk that accepts

signals from instruments, other line sources or microphones.

Interval (Major, Minor And Perfect) – The distance in pitch between two notes.

Inversion – A rearrangement of notes within a chord.

Key – A term that describe the seven different notes within a scale, all of which are then related to the starting note of that scale.

Key Signature – The complement of sharps or flats within a key.

Legato – Italian musical term meaning 'smoothly'.

Line Out – A socket or separate box that sends an electronic output signal via a lead.

Line Signal – An electronic audio signal sent through a cable.

Major – A specific arrangement of notes within a scale or chord, characterised by a sharpened third note.

Male – Describes a connection on a lead or socket of any type that has protruding pins to mate with a corresponding recessed (female) version.

MIDI Channels – The standard MIDI protocol allows data (such as note information) to be sent and received on 16 separate channels, all carried through a five-pin DIN cable.

MIDI File – A file containing MIDI information that should be able to be played as music on any GM (General MIDI)-equipped keyboard or module.

MIDI Interface – A panel on a piece of electronic music equipment that contains the MIDI sockets necessary to transmit and/or receive MIDI information.

MIDI Module – a keyboardless sound-generating unit that, in a playing environment, acts as a slave, triggered by another MIDI-equipped device, such as a keyboard.

Minimoog – A pioneering, compact 1960s monophonic synthesiser designed by Robert Moog.

Minor – A specific arrangement of notes within a scale or chord, characterised by a flattened third note.

Mono – Describes a system whereby identical audio signals are sent to both the left and right hand sides of a sound system, as opposed to stereo. (See *stereo*.)

Monophonic – describes the capability of an instrument to play only one note at a time.

Multitimbral – An instrument able to play several sounds at once (if required, on separate MIDI channels) is said to be multitimbral.

Natural – A sign (♮) which, when placed before a note, indicates that it should be played without accidentals, ie in its 'natural' form.

Note – A single sound of a particular pitch and length.

Octave – Two notes with the same key letter name that

are eight scale-based steps apart.

Pan – System of placing sounds within a left/right stereo image.

Piano – Italian musical term meaning 'quietly', pronounced 'pee-ah-no'.

Pitch – The description of how high or low a note is.

Polyphonic – Describes an instrument capable of playing several notes at one time.

Polyphony – The number of notes an instrument can play at one time.

Pulse – The feel of a beat that runs through a bar.

Quarter Note (Crotchet) – A note that is quarter the length of a whole note. In a bar of 4/4, there are four quarter notes to a bar.

Rallentando – Italian musical term meaning 'slow down'.

Root Position – Describes the position of a chord when the key note is at the bottom.

Scale – A succession of notes in ascending or descending steps.

Second Inversion – The second specific arrangement of notes in a chord when ascending from root position.

Semitone (Half Tone) – the distance between two adjacent notes in the 12-tone Western scale.

Sequencer – A device that allows the recording and playback of information, usually using MIDI signals to transmit and receive data. May be either a stand-alone hardware device, a software program or a facility built into a keyboard.

Sequencer Program – Software program operated on a computer that performs the same function as a sequencer.

Sharp – A sign (♯) which, when placed before a note, raises it by a semitone. When an instrument or voice is above the correct pitch, it is said to 'be sharp'.

Simple Time – Time signature in which each beat is divisible by two.

Slave – device or instrument that is controlled via MIDI by another MIDI-equipped device.

Soft Pedal – Left-hand pedal on a piano which has the effect of lessening the volume when the keys are depressed.

Stave – The five-line framework on which music that conforms to standard notation is written. Piano or keyboard music typically has two staves: one for the lower (left) hand and one for the upper (right) hand.

Stereo – Two-channel system capable of feeding different audio signals to both left and right loudspeakers.

Sustain Pedal – Pedal used in conjunction with a keyboard that holds on notes when depressed.

Time Signature – Description of the number of beats in a bar and the length of each beat.

Tone – An interval of two semitones.

Tonic – The key note (for instance C in the chord or key of C major) of a scale.

Transposing – The action of moving a note, chord, piece or section of music to another key. Electronic keyboards normally have a Transpose function, allowing the player to play in other keys while remaining in the same physical position on the keyboard.

Triad – A chord featuring the first, third and fifth notes of a major or minor scale.

USB – Abbreviation of Universal Serial Buss, an increasingly common interface connection between a computer and ancillary equipment.

Voice Reserve – Method of specifying the number of notes allowed to a particular part of a multitimbral keyboard.

AND FINALLY...

Here's a few words of wisdom from musical luminaries to inspire you in your music-making quest.

'I started making music because I could.' *Alanis Morissette*

'Music can name the unnameable and communicate the unknowable.' *Leonard Bernstein*

'Do you know that our soul is composed of harmony?' *Leonardo Da Vinci*

'Music can change the world.' *Ludwig Van Beethoven*

'Music is the universal language of mankind.' *Henry Wadsworth Longfellow*

'Music is enough for a lifetime – but a lifetime is not enough for music.' *Sergei Rachmaninoff*

'I saw my first Moog in a studio in London in the late '60s. It was a wonderful monster and I immediately fell in love with it and the phenomenal sounds it made.' *Rick Wakeman*

'How you develop your style? It's a matter of trying things and working it out.' *McCoy Tyner*

'I think that working with a lot of different artists and styles has helped me to define my own style.' *Liam Howlett, Prodigy*

'If true computer music was ever written, it would only be listened to by other computers.' *Michael Crichton*

APPENDIX
Quick-Reference Key-Signature Chart

73

NOTES

100 Tips For Keyboards You Should Have Been Told – **Part 1**

Also available from **smt**

PRO-SECRETS OF HEAVY ROCK SINGING

Bill Martin | £12.99 | $18.95 | 1-86074-437-0

100 GUITAR TIPS YOU SHOULD HAVE BEEN TOLD

David Mead | £20 | $21.95 | 1-86074-295-5

100 TIPS FOR ACOUSTIC GUITAR YOU SHOULD HAVE BEEN TOLD

David Mead | £20 | $21.95 | 1-86074-400-1

100 TIPS FOR BLUES GUITAR YOU SHOULD HAVE BEEN TOLD

David Mead | £19.99 | $24.95 | 1-84492-001-1

100 TIPS FOR DRUMS YOU SHOULD HAVE BEEN TOLD

Pete Riley | £19.99 | $24.95 | 1-86074-435-4

BASIC MIDI

Paul White | £5 | $7.95 | 1-86074-262-9

MIDI FOR THE TECHNOPHOBE (SECOND EDITION)

Paul White | £11.95 | $19.95 | 1-86074-444-3

GIANTS OF ROCK

Jamie Humphries | £19.99 | $24.95 | 1-86074-509-1

GIANTS OF BLUES

Neville Marten | £19.99 | $24.95 | 1-86074-211-4

HOW TO GET THE SOUND YOU WANT

Michael and Tim Prochak | £11.95 | $19.95 | 1-86074-348-X

RHYTHM PROGRAMMING

Mark Roberts | £11.95 | $19.95 | 1-86074-412-5

CUBASE SX - THE OFFICIAL GUIDE

Michael Prochak | £11.95 | $17.95 | 1-86074-470-2

MACWORLD MUSIC HANDBOOK

Michael Prochak | £20 | $28 | 1-86074-319-6

DESKTOP DIGITAL STUDIO

Paul White | £11.95 | $20 | 1-86074-324-2

FOR MORE INFORMATION on titles from Sanctuary Publishing visit our website at www.sanctuarypublishing.com or contact us at: Sanctuary House, 45-53 Sinclair Road, London W14 0NS. Tel: +44 (0)20 7602 6351

To order a title direct call our sales department or write to the above address. You can also order from our website at www.sanctuarypublishing.com